I0801400

IMAGINATION AND PARTICIPATION

Next Steps in Public Library Architecture

Joyce Sternheim & Rob Bruijnzeels

nai010 publishers

OVER

CONTENTS

VIEW

This book consists of six parts, each providing food for thought in the process of arriving at a new architecture for public libraries. You can browse through it in your own way. The first part about the transition that libraries are dealing with is followed with an elaboration of the value of the public library in a social and urban context. Next, we present an overview of library typologies that have inspired architects over the centuries. Part four of the book is devoted to the vision of the Ministry of Imagination and the associated new work process, based on the participation of library users. In part 5 valuable inspiration is offered by the conversations we had with architects. And finally, the last part of the book contains our 'Programme of Imagination': new principles for the architecture and design of public libraries, including a practical framework that will help architects and librarians to recognize and acknowledge their different perceptions and construct a successful design process.

Use this QR code to get more information about typologies, the sources we used, the libraries we mention and the architects we spoke with. Or go to: www.imaginationandparticipation.com

TRANSITION

I HAVE TO CHANGE TO STAY THE SAME

TRANSITION:
VALUE:
TYPOLOGY:
PARTICIPATION:
INSPIRATION:
IMAGINATION:

T

WHY THIS BOOK

'I HAVE TO CHANGE TO STAY THE SAME'

THIS FREQUENTLY QUOTED ADAGE IS ON THE WALL OF THE WILLEM DE KOONING ACADEMY OF ART AND DESIGN IN ROTTERDAM, THE NETHERLANDS. WILLEM DE KOONING, A ROTTERDAM PAINTER WHO EVENTUALLY SETTLED IN NEW YORK CITY, WAS ONE OF THE LEADING PROPONENTS OF ABSTRACT EXPRESSIONISM. DURING HIS LIFETIME, DE KOONING NEVER CEASED TO EXPLORE NEW STYLES AND METHODS, OFTEN CHALLENGING HIS OWN SKILLS AND ARTISTRY. HE FELT THAT THE ONLY WAY TO STAY TRUE TO HIS PASSION WAS TO CHANGE AND EVOLVE CONTINUALLY.

It's a brilliant motto that is equally applicable to the future strategy of public libraries. To stay relevant in today's society they urgently need to change, while retaining their core values and traditional strength. But what sort of change are we talking about, and what are the strengths and values that need to be preserved?

We've been researching these questions for quite some time, initially from our position as library consultants, but in recent years also from our growing interest in the architecture and design of public libraries. Because one thing soon became clear: the need to radically rethink the library will also irrevocably change how library space is arranged.

This insight led to the creation of the Ministry of Imagination, the think-tank and design collective we've been part of in recent years. Together with our colleagues from the Ministry we developed a new strategy for public libraries, supported by matching criteria for the use and layout of library space. This concept has been brought into practice in several libraries in the Netherlands and abroad.

Our search for answers didn't stop, though. Every time a new prestigious library was opened anywhere in the world, we were keen to know about the underlying ideas. Was it the last of the old libraries or the first of the new? So, we decided to start a series of conversations with renowned Dutch and Flemish architects who have designed public libraries in both the Netherlands and abroad. We particularly wanted to know whether they believed the changing role of public libraries in society could lead to a new typology, a unique building type, with its own architectural principles. We also wanted to find out how the architects had experienced the collaboration with the librarian. Did the library itself come up with a clear vision? And were the architects able to match this with their own ideas?

Michel Melot, director of the Centre Pompidou Library in Paris, once said: 'Every librarian is, up to a certain point, an architect. He builds up his collection as an ensemble through which the reader must find a path, discover his own self, and live.[1]' The question is, of course, whether librarians and architects share the same perception of what a library should look like. They might use the same words, but mean something different. It brings to mind the rabbit-duck illusion that was made famous by Ludwig Wittgenstein. In his 'Philosophical Investigations' he used this as an example of a form that can be perceived in different ways and thus allows different interpretations.

In addition to the conversations with the architects, we talked to experts in the field of public space and urban planning. As we mainly focus on city libraries, we wanted to learn more about the potential of public libraries to serve as catalysts in the social, cultural, and economic revival of urban areas. Nowadays it's increasingly common for library building projects to be part of urban development plans, as was the case in the cities of Amsterdam, Århus, Ghent, and Helsinki. Inspired by all the conversations we had and the new insights we gained, we decided to publish this book. It's a first, because up till now there hasn't been a book that specifically deals with the architecture of public libraries. Existing books on library architecture make no distinction between public, special, or academic libraries. 'A library is a library', the motto seems to be. However, unlike special and academic libraries, public libraries have a social mission. As the name already implies, they serve the general public and support people of all ages and backgrounds in developing the skills they need to thrive in today's society. In line with this mission, the collection of the public library differs from that of special or academic libraries. In order to serve the diversity of people and cultures in the local community, it needs to reflect a variety of ideas, information, stories, and experiences.

Due to their social mission and focus on the general public, the business processes of public libraries are fundamentally different from those of special and academic libraries. Since architecture is often the physical representation of a work process, it is obvious that the architecture of public libraries requires a different approach than that of specialized and academic libraries. In short, it's time for a book specifically devoted to public library architecture. An architecture that celebrates the core values of the public library by providing reading and study opportunities, while at the same time creating space for real change: new forms of knowledge development through interaction and challenging programming. With this book we aim to inspire librarians, architects, planners, and policy makers to bring about a truly innovative architecture that represents the distinctive and active forms of knowledge development and sharing that take place in public libraries. The guideline we follow in our search for answers consists of three elements: identifying social changes, analyzing their impact on public libraries, and deriving new design principles from that. In addition, you can read about the visions and ideas of the architects and the other experts we spoke with.
And in the end we will combine all this with our own insights and practical experiences to subsequently draw up new principles for the architecture and design of public libraries.

> Academic libraries serve colleges and universities, their students, staff, and faculty. Larger institutions may have several libraries on their campuses dedicated to serving particular schools such as law and science libraries.
> Public libraries serve communities of all sizes and types. As the name implies, public libraries serve the general public, "from cradle to grave", as more than one public librarian has been heard to say.
> Special libraries are operating in a specialized environment of interest, such as corporations, hospitals, the military, museums, private businesses, and the government.
>
> http://www.ala.org/educationcareers/careers/librarycareerssite/typesoflibraries

1 Michel Melot. La Sagesse du bibliothécaire (Paris: L'oeil neuf éditions, 2004) p. 70

WHAT'S GOING ON?

THE REVIVAL OF THE PUBLIC LIBRARY

Public libraries are experiencing a renaissance. For a long time, the prevailing opinion was that library buildings would become obsolete by the increasing digitization of information. Nothing could be further from the truth. Visitor numbers continue to grow and there's an increasing awareness that public libraries play a vital role in the social, cultural, and economic vitality of communities.

All over the world, impressive and often even iconic new library buildings are being built, often designed by famous architects. The question is whether these spectacular buildings truly represent a new vision of the role of the public library. And if they do, how is this vision reflected in the architecture of the building? We see futuristic buildings that, on closer inspection, are quite traditionally furnished. The archetype of the library in ultra-modern packaging, you could say. On the other hand, we have encountered beautiful buildings that are able to accommodate a wide range of activities, but are hardly recognizable as a library because the collection has been given a minor role. Sometimes it seems as if an existing typology of the library was the starting point of the design process, while in other cases every attempt was made to avoid the traditional image of the library. Such divergent interpretations can be considered illustrative of the public library's quest for a new identity. A quest that largely stems from the exponential growth of the internet and social media.

FACING THE DIGITAL AGE

For the majority of people, the internet and online social networks have become the primary sources of information. It's where people express their opinions and add their own content, resulting in an overload of information. These developments have an enormous impact on public libraries. The traditional process of distributing information by selecting media and making them accessible to the public is no longer deemed to be sufficient, as the information overload gives rise to a growing need for interpretation and meaning.

In response, libraries are placing great emphasis on supporting people to develop digital skills. Necessary and important, but is it an adequate answer to developments in society? In our opinion, these skills mainly contribute to people's ability to take care of themselves as individuals. Getting people to actively participate in society is a different story. A vital society requires social responsibility, a willingness to seek knowledge, respect for other people's opinions, and the ability to collaborate on problem-solving.

Precisely these values are in danger of being lost in the digital age. Since algorithms determine what you get to see on the web or in your newsfeed, you are presented with information that mainly supports your own opinions and perspectives. As a result, a disturbing phenomenon occurs: people increasingly become isolated within their own bubble of like-minded people, excluding themselves from encountering different views and ideas.

THE NEED FOR COLLECTIVE INTELLIGENCE

We started writing this book in the middle of the Covid-19 pandemic, a dramatic time in which it became even more apparent how public opinion is influenced by the internet and social media. We were inundated with fake news and conspiracy theories, resulting in increased polarization, while more than ever we craved solidarity and the collective intelligence of communities.

The Covid-19 crisis is an extreme example, of course, but it undeniably demonstrates how important it is to involve people in problems and topics that affect their lives and their local communities and stimulate them to jointly come up with smart and creative solutions.

We need 'the creative intelligence of communities' or the 'Scenius' as it is called by musician and producer Brian Eno. He introduced this term to counter the idea that innovation in art and culture comes from geniuses working in solitude, when in reality great ideas are often spawned by a group of creative individuals. For him, it simply confirms that good work does not come in a vacuum, and that creativity is always, in a sense, a collaboration, the result of a mind connected to other minds.

The core idea is that people with different interests, different ideas, backgrounds, and opinions, enter into a conversation about a theme or issue, in order to ultimately arrive at a creative solution. It's important to realize that this is not about bringing together like-minded people. Everyone should be able to participate, regardless of cultural background or educational level. As Brian Eno puts it in his explanation of the Scenius, it's not about how smart you are, but about what you have to contribute: 'the ideas you share, the quality of the connections you make and the conversations you start.' It's another step libraries need to take: instead of just focusing on the skills people lack - the so-called deficit model - they should recognize that people can have many other talents and abilities that allow them to make a positive contribution to their communities.

As they are the most visited public facilities, reaching all sections of the population, public libraries are ideal places for the development of the Scenius, the creative intelligence of local communities. They provide a rich and stimulating environment that creates the perfect conditions for exchanging knowledge, ideas, and personal stories. Not just because you can meet people face-to-face and have spontaneous as well as organized encounters, but also because you are surrounded by essential sources of knowledge and inspiration: the library collection.

> "NEW LIBRARIES DON'T REINVENT OR EVEN MODERNIZE THE TRADITIONAL INSTITUTION; THEY MERELY PACKAGE IT IN A NEW WAY"

From Seattle Public Library Proposal, OMA (1999)

WHAT IS THE SAME AND WHAT IS THE CHANGE?

THE NEXT STEP

Public libraries strive to enrich, empower, and inspire people in order to support their full participation in society. This is predominantly accomplished by giving people access to sources of information, knowledge and culture and providing them with the necessary skills to use these sources in an effective way. Going back to Willem de Kooning's statement, this should definitely stay the same. But it should not be left at that. Our rapidly changing society calls for a library that reflects today's need for development and innovation; a library of the people and of the community they are part of. It requires the library to transform into a dynamic and active social setting, that is not just aimed at educating individuals, but at supporting the community as a whole. Therefore, the next step for the library should be: expanding the focus from lifelong learning to lifelong participation.

LIFELONG PARTICIPATION

The skills and knowledge required to function in a society change continuously. That's why people need to keep on learning even after their formal education is completed. Public libraries have an important role in promoting lifelong learning by supporting essential skills, such as digital and media literacy, and the ability to find a job, understand finances, live a healthy life, and so on. In our opinion, however, the purpose of lifelong learning is primarily expressed in economic terms, while there is also a clear relationship with civic literacy: the knowledge, skills, and mentality necessary for active and engaged citizenship. Being an active citizen means to have a sense of belonging to a community, feeling solidarity and responsibility for the people in that community, respecting their opinions and being willing to collaborate on issues of mutual concern. As we mentioned earlier, the skills and attitudes required for active citizenship are becoming less common in the digital age. The internet and social media tend to reinforce opinions without empathy and consideration for personal circumstances and arguments. To reach mutual understanding and find solutions together people need to meet face-to-face and enter into a real dialogue.

We think public libraries should play an important role in promoting active citizenship by addressing topics and encouraging conversations in their local communities. Enabling co-creation is inextricably linked to that. And last but not least, the collection, an established asset of the public library, should be given a more active role in fostering individual and collective intelligence.

FROM PERSONAL DEVELOPMENT TO COMMUNITY DEVELOPMENT

Personal development can no longer be seen in isolation. Exchanging thoughts and ideas is essential in the process of gaining knowledge and insight, so instead of just 'consuming' information, people need to be engaged in real dialogue. By stimulating conversations, the library enables people to explore different interpretations of facts and events. This will not only help them establish their own point of view, but will also enhance the development of knowledge and shared understanding in the community.

TOWARDS CREATIVE INVOLVEMENT

Traditional library processes, such as collection development and cataloguing, no longer provide an adequate response to these developments. The library will increasingly have to take on a coordinating and inspiring role in the process of knowledge creation and exchange. In an era of co-creation, the knowledge and expertise of users will be indispensable to this role. It means the library must establish a new relationship with its users. They can no longer be looked upon just as consumers, but must also be recognized as editors and producers of information, knowledge, and stories in whatever form. The library has to tap into the collective insight of people and allow their knowledge and activities to become part of the library collection.

A RENEWED APPRECIATION OF THE COLLECTION

Digital technology has not replaced print media, and will not do so in the foreseeable future either. Strangely enough, though, it is often librarians themselves who question the importance of physical library collections. 'It's not about books anymore' is a statement we've come across several times. And sometimes they even add the predicate 'dusty', to discredit the books even more.

It is as if the fear of being taken for old-fashioned leads to the importance of the collection being marginalized. This is probably motivated by the idea that the necessity to change is first and foremost caused by the transition from physical to digital information. We believe, however, that the real challenge lies in adding context and meaning, enabling co-creation and establishing connections in the community. And it is precisely the collection, comprising both print media and electronic sources, that can play an active role in this.

WHAT THIS FOR PUBLIC ARCHITECT

It's clear that public libraries will have to develop new processes to engage people in face-to-face conversations and enable them to exchange knowledge and insight and add new content to the collection. But how will these processes manifest themselves in the library building of the future?
In the past, library space was primarily defined by the number of bookcases and how they were arranged. Now we literally need to make way for new forms of meaningful interaction between users and between users and the collection. It's a fundamental reform that goes beyond creating a welcoming space that is accessible to everyone. In order to stimulate participation and citizenship the library must actively challenge people to join discussions, add their own knowledge and experience and come up with new ideas that become part of the collection and are shared within the community. This calls for a library that triggers curiosity and encourages reflection - an environment that is thought-provoking and sometimes even a bit disruptive, with a prominent role for the collection.
But what design principles can be derived from that? And how can they be put into practice, taking into account that there's no such thing as a one-size-fits-all model? To find answers, we definitely need a generous amount of creativity and imagination, as well as the expertise of architects and specialists in cultural placemaking.

MEANS
LIBRARY
URE

VALUE

CATHEDRALS OF THE MIND;
HOSPITALS OF THE SOUL;
THEME PARKS OF THE IMAGINATION'

TRANSITION:
VALUE:
TYPOLOGY:
PARTICIPATION:
INSPIRATION:
IMAGINATION:

V

WHAT MAKES PUBLIC LIBRARIES UNIQUE?

Maybe it's best to leave the imagining of a public library to writers...

THE VALUE OF THE LIBRARY IN A SOCIAL AND URBAN CONTEXT

CAITLIN MORAN, ENGLISH JOURNALIST, AUTHOR, AND COLUMNIST FOR THE TIMES, HAS DONE A REMARKABLE JOB OF ARTICULATING THE ROLE THE LIBRARY CAN PLAY IN THE COMMUNITY AND IN PEOPLE'S LIVES. IN ONE OF HER COLUMNS ABOUT THE IMPORTANCE OF LIBRARIES, SHE WROTE: 'A LIBRARY IN THE MIDDLE OF A COMMUNITY IS A CROSS BETWEEN AN EMERGENCY EXIT, A LIFE RAFT AND A FESTIVAL. THEY ARE CATHEDRALS OF THE MIND; HOSPITALS OF THE SOUL; THEME PARKS OF THE IMAGINATION. ON A COLD, RAINY ISLAND, THEY ARE THE ONLY SHELTERED PUBLIC SPACES WHERE YOU ARE NOT A CONSUMER, BUT A CITIZEN, INSTEAD. A HUMAN WITH A BRAIN AND A HEART AND A DESIRE TO BE UPLIFTED, RATHER THAN A CUSTOMER WITH A CREDIT CARD AND AN INCHOATE "NEED" FOR STUFF.'[1]

IT IS A BEAUTIFUL DESCRIPTION, BUT ONE THAT ALSO IMMEDIATELY RAISES QUESTIONS. FOR WHAT IS IT THAT MAKES THE LIBRARY SUCH AN IMPORTANT PART OF THE COMMUNITY? TO WHAT DISTINCTIVE QUALITIES CAN THIS IMPORTANCE BE ATTRIBUTED, AND CAN WE MAKE THOSE CHARACTERISTICS EVEN MORE EXPLICIT IN ORDER TO EMPHASIZE THE LIBRARY'S UNIQUE POSITION IN SOCIETY AND IN THE URBAN ENVIRONMENT?

MORE THAN A MEETING PLACE

The library is one of the few truly public places left in our society. A freely accessible, non-commercial place where people from all walks of life can meet face-to-face.

The role of the library as a public meeting place is therefore used as an important argument in discussions about the social relevance of the library. In our opinion, this argument can be strengthened even more if we stress not only the importance of meeting, but also the importance of interaction, of exchange between people. Meeting does not automatically lead to the exchange of knowledge, ideas, and inspiration that is so instrumental to the development of collective intelligence. It needs something that triggers people's curiosity and reflection, something that encourages conversation. And what is so unique about the library is that it can actively use its collection for this purpose.

1 Libraries: Cathedrals of Our Souls by Caitlin Moran, The Huffington Post, November 14, 2012. https://www.huffpost.com/entry/libraries-cathedrals-of-o_b_2103362?utm_hp_ref=books. Previously published in The Times, and included in Moran, Caitlin (2012). Moranthology. London, Ebury Press.

THE VITAL ROLE OF THE COLLECTION

A library collection, comprising both print media and electronic sources, often including special collections of local records and artifacts, is an indispensable source of information and inspiration when it comes to stimulating creativity and tackling themes and issues that are of interest to the local community.
A well-curated collection contains a wide range of expressions, opinions, and views, providing the context that is now so often lost, due to the dominance of the polarized debate on social media. And it is decidedly not just the non-fiction collection that provides this context. The stories being told in novels, films, and even in music, are essentially explorations of human history and experience that will help us understand other people's perspectives and develop empathic skills.
To initiate a meaningful exchange of knowledge and ideas, the library should actively challenge people to engage in conversations and discuss issues that are of interest to the local community, using the collection to provide the necessary context. The fact that these discussions will sometimes be accompanied by friction actually helps in discovering new perspectives and solutions.
This calls for an environment where different opinions are allowed to coexist; a place where people feel free to engage in conversation and reach mutual understanding, while being surrounded by essential sources of knowledge and inspiration: the library collection.

ROOM FOR DISPUTE

Face-to-face meeting and interaction are indispensable when it comes to reaching mutual understanding and agreement. Maarten Hajer, Professor of Urban Futures at Utrecht University, also stresses this. In an interview we had with him, he described physical encounters, exchanges in a non-threatening way, as crucial for a resilient society. He argues that a city where it is not possible for people from different backgrounds to meet each other soon becomes an archipelago of enclaves. For him, this goes to the heart of the matter: there have to be places where moments of friction can arise.
In connection with this, he used the term 'agonistic democracy', a democracy in which people look for solutions together, without avoiding disagreements. The Belgian political theorist Chantal Mouffe introduced this concept as a counterpart to the consensus model. She argues that we should accept the fact that people can have different opinions. It is not about who is right or wrong, but about exchanging the underlying arguments. She believes that there should be room for disputes, not to face each other as enemies, but to engage in a respectful debate based on values such as freedom and equality.
On this subject Maarten said: 'If you want the library to be a place of agonistic democracy, a space that feels safe enough for people to be themselves and to share their opinions with others in a conversation, then you have to work towards a building in which—apart from the collection that you make serviceable to that conversation—you also expressively give that exchange a place'.

A BIGGER IMAGINATION

We also believe that libraries need bigger imaginations. The classic function of the library is to work on emancipation, on public edification. But—as Maarten Hajer puts it—it is also about the question: how do you get people to dare to imagine that life could be better? Not by increasing their assets, but by taking control of their daily lives. Our cities lack places that are suitable for this.

We come across a similar point of view with Eric Klinenberg, sociology professor at New York University and author of Palaces for the people.[1] The title of his book is taken from Andrew Carnegie, the Scottish-American industrialist and philanthropist who funded more than 2500 libraries around the world, calling them 'palaces for the people'. According to Klinenberg, the library is literally 'your palace where you could make something of yourself. A place where you experience the sense of opportunity and are inspired to become something greater.'

THE 'OTHER PLACE'

The library as a place where people can walk in with the idea that they can grow, and give new direction to their lives. Where they get the feeling that they together constitute society, and see a role for themselves in it... How can we best characterize such a place?
It is clear that the still very popular description of the library as a casual meeting place or 'Third Place'[2] no longer suffices. After all, in a building where many people come together, social interaction and a sense of community do not develop automatically.

1 Eric Klinenberg. Palaces for the people: a plea for social infrastructure as a means to fight inequality, polarization, and the decline of civic life. New York, Crown, 2018.

2 The term Third Place was first introduced by the American urban sociologist Ray Oldenburg in his book The Great Good Place (1989). He defines the Third Place as the place separate from home and work or school, where people come together in an informal way, 'where you relax in public, where you encounter familiar faces and make new acquaintances'.

A characterization that does more justice to the meaning and complexity of what takes place in the library is 'heterotopia', which literally means 'other place'. The philosopher Michel Foucault coined this term to describe places reserved for something special, out of the ordinary. It is an in-between space, a place where you can develop yourself, and where your perspective can change through interaction with other people and other cultural expressions. The 'library as heterotopia', in our view, is then a building that you enter with the aim of being transformed, which ties in with Foucault's statement that 'The main interest in life and work is to become someone else that you were not in the beginning'.[3]
Heterotopia thus refers both to an environment that is stimulating and enriching for your development and to a place of interaction where the different worlds of community members meet.

THE LIBRARY IN THE URBAN ENVIRONMENT

Heterotopia, 'the other place', which is all about interaction and transformation, demands new ways of working that irrevocably affect the architecture and layout of the building. But it also raises the question of how such a building fits into a city. Can the library earn its own place in the urban infrastructure in this way? And how do you then convince other parties of the importance of the library for that urban society?

A new public library is a guaranteed crowd-puller, but it has to hold its own amidst other cultural and commercial parties in the urban environment. This means that you have to be able to explain very well what purpose you have in mind as a library, and why that function is important at that particular location in the city.

Creative producer Marjo van Schaik, who obtained her PhD in 2018 with research on new buildings and the redevelopment of cultural buildings in Amsterdam,[4] agrees that it is more important than ever that the library shows what role it fulfills in society, and what its distinguishing qualities are. In her research, she found that cultural institutions do have a vision, but that generic concepts such as open, transparent, and accessible predominate. The true identity of the institutions is usually not adequately expressed. Why do they exist, what is their role or mission, and how do they want to fulfil it? These are core questions that require an in-depth exploration, because a truly fitting architecture can only follow in conjunction with these questions.
Marjo also stresses that more attention should be paid to participation, and what exactly is meant by it. Many institutions say they are open to participation and co-creation, while in practice they come up with all the activities themselves, with the aim of bringing in as many people as possible, and thus creating as much turnover as possible. Such an attitude is not appropriate for an institution with an idealistic objective, such as the library.

A complicating factor is that the construction of a new library is now often part of an urban development project. As a librarian, you then find yourself in a complex interplay with other parties, some of whom may have idealistic objectives too, but others may have commercial aims. It is then even more important to know what objective you have in mind, what you want to mean for the local population, and with whom you intend to collaborate. The right considerations and choices can only be made based on a vision that provides support and direction. But it also requires expertise that you, as a librarian, don't necessarily have. According to Marjo, in the first, crucial phase of such a development project, it is important for the library to engage not only a financial adviser but also an urban planner. The urban planner can assess whether the vision the library has in mind will actually come into its own on the site it has been allocated. In the follow-up phase, when the choice of an architect has been made, that in-depth exploration will follow, in which the architect and the library together will arrive at a design that reflects the library's unique identity and is best suited to the location and the needs of the local population.

How important this local context is for the final result is evidenced by the success of two recent Dutch libraries: Forum in Groningen and LocHal in Tilburg. They show that even in a small country such as the Netherlands, the character of cities can differ so much that two completely different library buildings arise, both of which fit perfectly into their surroundings.

3 Foucault, M. (1988), 'Truth, power, self: an interview with Michel Foucault', in Martin, L.H., Gutman, H. and Hutton, P.H. (Eds), Technologies of the Self: A Seminar with Michel Foucault, University of Massachusetts Press, Amherst, MA, pp. 9-15.

4 Spaces of Culture. New cultural venues in Amsterdam: research and strategies. Rotterdam, nai010 publishers, 2018.

In our conversations with architects, it was repeatedly mentioned that public libraries often serve as a catalyst for urban development projects. This certainly applies to the development of what are called 'the fringes' of the city: unattractive or newly developed areas in a city where few people come. Libraries are usually the most visited cultural institutions in a city and therefore guarantee a decent amount of traffic. This also makes it attractive for other (commercial) parties to invest in such an area: shops, restaurants, houses, et cetera.

Here are some examples of twenty-first-century public libraries that play an important role in urban development:

CITY AND COUNTRY	LIBRARY	ARCHITECT
AMSTERDAM (NL)	OBA	JO COENEN
STUTTGART (DE)	STADTBIBLIOTHEK	YI ARCHITECTS
ARNHEM (NL)	ROZET	NEUTELINGS RIEDIJK ARCHITECTS
ÅRHUS (DK)	DOKK1	SCHMIDT HAMMER LASSEN ARCHITECTS
GENT (BE)	DE KROOK	COUSSÉE & GORIS AND RCR ARQUITECTES
AALST (BE)	UTOPIA	KAAN ARCHITECTS
HELSINKI (FI)	OODI	ALA ARCHITECTS
TILBURG (NL)	LOCHAL	CIVIC ARCHITECTS AND BRAAKSMA & ROOS ARCHITECTS

LIBRARIES AND URBAN

YEAR OF CONSTRUCTION	URBAN PLANNING PROJECT
2007	DEVELOPMENT OOSTERDOKS ISLAND
2011	STUTTGART 21: REDEVELOPMENT FORMER RAILWAY YARD
2013	REGENERATION CITY CENTRE (MASTERPLAN RIJNBOOG)
2015	DEVELOPMENT HARBOUR FRONT
2017	DEVELOPMENT 'WAALSE KROOK' AREA
2018	CONNECTION STATION AREA AND CITY CENTRE
2018	REDEVELOPMENT FORMER RAILWAY YARD
2019	DEVELOPMENT SPOORZONE (FORMER DUTCH RAILWAYS MAINTENANCE SITE)

CASE STUDY

GESAM KUNST

Forum

OR TO

T-
WERK

How different urban contexts
led to two very different libraries:

roningen & LocHal Tilburg

OLBOX

TijdLab

It seemed to go on and on:

two years in a row, a public library building won just about every architecture prize there was to win in the Netherlands. The LocHal in Tilburg, which opened at the beginning of 2019, was even named World Building of the Year. A year later, Forum Groningen was awarded the prize for Building of the Year 2020 by the Branchevereniging van Nederlandse Architectenbureaus (Dutch Architects' Association), the building 'with the most added value for clients and society'. Perhaps even more remarkable was the fact that architecture critics and visitors were all in agreement. The LocHal (construction and interior € 34.5 million) and the Forum (construction and interior approximately € 100 million, of which € 25 million was used to make the building earthquake-proof) became popular and well-visited buildings from the first day they opened their doors, making the local residents happy and proud.

What is the secret of these buildings, which were immediately embraced by the residents, and became the most important meeting places in the city from the moment they opened? And what are the similarities and differences?

We can certainly see similarities. Both cities have about 200,000 inhabitants, and are considered typical educational cities with colleges and a university. What is also striking is the similarity in the urban planning context. Neither Tilburg nor Groningen had a problem with existing library buildings. Their libraries were housed in modern buildings, which were centrally located in the cities' shopping districts. Perhaps they were no longer entirely up-to-date, but certainly neither situation was so dramatic as to warrant a new building. The two cities had different problems, though. Groningen wanted to redevelop the east side of the Grote Markt, an area that had been left with poor architectural quality in the recovery period after the Second World War. Tilburg was looking for a new use for the LocHal, a former Dutch Railways maintenance site, dating from 1932. This monumental train depot had not been in use since 2011, and was part of the Railway zone, a 'forbidden city' at the edge of the city centre that was virtually closed to the public.

Both Groningen and Tilburg opted for the construction of a new public library as a catalyst for area development. A notable difference being that Groningen gave the library a new location in the city centre, whereas Tilburg chose to take the library out of the commercial environment of the city centre to spark the development of the Railway zone, turning it into a new creative hub.

In both cases, the choice led to high-profile and spectacular libraries, which is a great compliment to the courage and vision of these libraries to leave their safe, old environment, and embark on a new—and at the time uncertain—adventure. An adventure that eventually turned into a success story. This great success is all the more remarkable because, on closer inspection, the approach and design of the buildings are diametrically opposed. Is there more than one road to success after all?

The buildings had different programmes. In Tilburg, the library is unmistakably the main occupant: 11,200 square metres on three floors in a sturdy, industrial hall with clear sightlines. In contrast, Forum Groningen houses several complementary partners: a library, a cinema complex, a city shop, and a museum of comics and games. A total of 17,500 square metres, built on a small plot in the middle of the city. This results in an exciting and striking building, which rises like a medieval cathedral: 45 metres high with 10 floors, 'split level', all connected by escalators. This makes the libraries very different from each other in terms of typology: LocHal is set up like an open terrace landscape; Forum can best be characterized as an intricate city with streets, squares, and even alleys.

However, the differences are not only limited to building and typology; the way the library functions are manifested in both buildings is also different. As soon as you enter the LocHal, you see the collection: you immediately know you are in a library, and that is a very deliberate choice. Peter Kok, director of the LocHal: 'We thought the worst thing would be if someone entering our building for the first time would say: "What a nice building, but what is it exactly?"' And indeed, there is not a single place in the LocHal where you cannot see the collection. The big risk with such a massive building volume as the LocHal is that the visitor becomes intimidated, and feels small and insignificant. But the architects did a fantastic job of eliminating that danger by cutting across the full width of the building with a clear and inviting staircase landscape that connects everything, and makes the building instantly comprehensible and accessible. The set of broad steps is both a connecting zone and a large terrace, a study area and a meeting area, and functions as the powerful spatial 'interface' of the LocHal. Flexibility is the magic word, and this effect is reinforced by the application of Petra Blaisse's[1] 'tactile architecture': six gigantic textile curtains (the largest one measures 47 by 15 metres), which can be used to compartmentalize and programme the space. Petra Blaisse herself says: 'We are good at making flexible rooms and movable screens with the help of curtains, so that's how this idea came about: a very spatial staircase landscape with six curtain cascades.'[2]

1 Petra Blaisse is a British born Dutch designer. In 1991 she founded Inside Outside, a design agency that specializes in landscape design and interior architecture.

2 Bibliotheekblad (1) 2020, 1 p 40 - 43.

What makes it extra special is that the curtains are a reference to Tilburg's past as a textile city. The curtains were even woven by the Textile Museum in Tilburg. Essential to the LocHal's formula of a 'house for knowledge and stories' are its six thematic 'labs' (technology, history, food, the city, games, and literature), which challenge visitors to use the collection creatively themselves. These labs are not hidden away in the edges of the building, but spread throughout the building. This spatial and programmatic integration underlines the industrial character of the LocHal, where everything revolves around the concepts of 'workshop, collection, and stage'.[3]
When you enter the Forum, you have to look for the collection, which you then find while strolling through the different streets and stacked squares of the building. In addition to the architecture of the building, with its spectacular, ever-changing sightlines, the interior design concept by the architects' collective deMunnik-deJong-Steinhauser also plays a key role. They have given each of the streets and squares a pleasant and surprising variety with their own thematic look and feel. They have certainly not opted for the uniformity of long, monotonous rows of bookcases. Instead, an optimal connection was sought with the various partners. For example, the film collection has been placed near the cinema, and the comic book collection near the entrance of the comics museum. A tour of the Forum is a great voyage of discovery, with the building and its interior as the main attractions: all equally beautiful, all custom-made. The disadvantage of such a beautifully 'styled' layout is probably that the library is less flexible in responding to future developments, other interests of the public, or new ideas about library work. On the other hand, the Forum has become a truly modern version of a Gesamtkunstwerk, where all the details are right: pleasant and seductive; perhaps even a bit vain....
The emphasis of the Forum is not on creation, but rather on being there, and this takes on an added dimension on the top floor, where the roof terrace provides a truly magnificent view of the city. From there, it is all the more striking how beautifully the building has been integrated into the historical city centre.
Two award-winning libraries, both completed in the same year, and yet completely different. Perhaps these differences ultimately account for their most important similarity, namely that both buildings perfectly reflect the character of the two cities. In the Forum, elegant, urban Groningen has gained a stylish element of vertical city centre, while the soul of raw, industrial Tilburg comes into its own in the fantastic toolbox that is the LocHal.
And so, the LocHal could never have been placed in Groningen and the Forum would be out of place in Tilburg. They are two striking and unique libraries, both exactly where they should be.

CONVERSATIONS WITH THE ARCHITECTS

The following is a photo overview of both libraries, along with information distilled from conversations we had with CIVIC (LocHal) and NL-architects (Forum).

3 Beleidsplan 2016-2019 Bibliotheek Midden Brabant. https://www.bibliotheeknieuwestijl.nl/beleidsplan/beleidsplan-overzicht/

KennisMakerij

CIVIC

Excerpts from a conversation with Gert Kwekkeboom and Rick ten Doeschate of CIVIC, architects of the Tilburg LocHal.

ABOUT THE DESIGN PHILOSOPHY

Gert: 'We founded CIVIC based on the idea that architecture and society are always interconnected, and that they inspire and influence each other. As an architect you cannot just ignore trends and social needs. That is, in a broad sense, why we design all kinds of public buildings. Not only government buildings or public buildings, but also other buildings that are relevant to large groups of people. CIVIC refers to civilian, in other words: for the citizen.'
Rick: 'We don't have one single conception of what public space should be. It is interesting to constantly re-examine what the function of that space should be in a particular building, or in a public place. What relationship do you want to establish between that space and the people who come in and use it? And what architectural means should you then use to define or strengthen that relationship?
It is characteristic of our office that we constantly analyse what is going on in such a specific case, what we think should happen and how we can create the desired situation.'
Rick: 'In any case, what we are aiming for is architecture that has a certain atmospheric, sensory quality, and is splendid in its materials, with great attention to detail. It is important that public buildings communicate in a certain way. They not only accommodate activities, but also tell us something about their function, and perhaps even about society. We are trying to find out how to give shape to this today, because there is no longer an architectural language that everyone understands. Secondly, we always look back in time, in the history of architecture: what has been done before, and how can we distill principles from that, to which we can then give an innovative twist? The third is: if it is a building in which different functions come together, then people must be able to make a space their own. At the same time, you want a building to continue to radiate collective strength, and to retain a certain calm and clarity. The tension between the two and finding the balance are also very much in our minds. Creating very clear structures, and accentuating them architecturally.'

ABOUT THE PUBLIC LIBRARY

Rick: 'The library is partly based on the principle that you don't just come there to consume knowledge, but perhaps also to bring something yourself. That places different demands on such a space.'
Gert: 'You expect something from people, but pushing them is never fun, of course. There are fewer and fewer public buildings where you can go without having to do anything. The church was always a place where everyone could walk in and out freely. The town hall, too, was a place where everyone came from time to time. These days, such buildings are increasingly secured and churches have become less public, so that people only go there for a specific purpose, when they have an appointment for example. This does not apply to libraries, which makes them attractive to a large audience. We sometimes talk about this among ourselves: what kind of buildings have such a wide audience as a library?'

ABOUT THE LOCHAL

Gert: 'The LocHal is a hard and rhythmic building with large surfaces and heavy columns. Suitable for the scale, because so much is going to happen in that building that it could use a sturdy frame. And then within that frame, a lot of things have to happen too. We try to keep this in balance in every project: a basic, almost simple and clear structure, and a refined interpretation.'
Rick: 'The special thing about this library is that different functions come together, and that there is not only an oversizing in terms of spaciousness, but also in the number of square metres. It becomes an almost monumental public interior, an extension of the public space in the city. At the same time, there is that human scale, because you can also find a place where you can just sit down and read a book.'
'The sensory experience of space is very important to us. That is what makes a physical space a thousand times better. Apart from your eyes, your senses are not stimulated all that much in the digital world, so that's something we like to explore, because we believe it makes people feel good.'
'It also touches on what we were just talking about: how to combine monumentality with the human scale. It is not just about proportions and what you see. All your senses play a part in it, so this has to be given careful consideration.'
Gert: 'That it gets brighter as you go up in the building, for example. We have positioned the quieter functions

there, so that you can work in a serene environment with lots of light. Downstairs, where the space is somewhat heavier and darker, is also where most of the hubbub will be. We have coordinated these things programmatically, and we believe that it will work.'

Rick: 'What makes this library so special in terms of typology is the combination with other functions. And also the presence of that large city hall, which can be used partly by the library, and partly by the other partners. That begs the question: What should such a building look like? Should it have a neutral look, because there are different users, and so it may not look one hundred percent like a library? In any case, it is not a traditional library, where the book is the architectural presence. The LocHal is an old industrial hall that will generate new knowledge. Programming is becoming increasingly important in this respect. What events do you organize during the year, what moments to share knowledge? In that open landscape, it is preferable not to arrange the collection according to the SISO [numerical library classification system]. That does not fit with curating and combining knowledge. Perhaps you should put everything with a thematic relation together. If all goes well, there will be a cooking lab, where cooking workshops will be held. Then you can organize your collection of cookery books around it, but also everything that has to do with health, food, and hospitality.'

NL Architects

Excerpts from a conversation with Kamiel Klaasse and Pieter Bannenberg of NL Architects, designers of the Groningen Forum.

ABOUT THE MIX OF FUNCTIONS IN THE FORUM

'We are always looking for certain crossovers in our work. Bringing things together in an interesting way, creating added value.'

'From the beginning, it was clear that the Forum would be a very special mix of things that had not been brought together before. Our design really catered to that, stimulated that mix.'

ABOUT THE DESIGN

'The text for the competition, called it a Wikipedia palace. Not aimed at searching but at finding.'

'If you want to make an efficient building, you can put all the escalators right on top of each other, and lead people straight to their destination. We have laid out the escalators in such a way that you come across all kinds of things along the way. It's a longer route to take, but it's purposefully been included in the design from day one.'

'In presentations, we often show the building from a bird's-eye view. People then say: what a colossal building, have they gone completely mad?

And the funny thing is, when they go there, they can't find the building right away. That's a good one. Searching for the building when you felt it was too big for that location.'

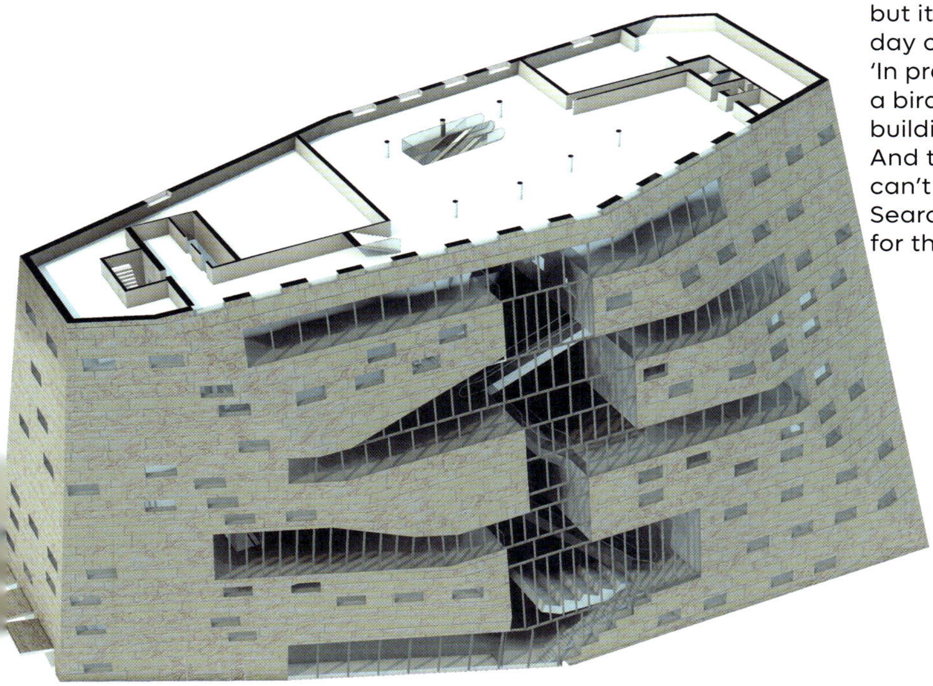

VAPIANO
VPLEGT-VOS
COMBISAFE

Liften OOST
Toilet
Verschoonruimte
Toilet via lift
LENEN
NIEUW

WOW
ACTUEEL
ACTUEEL

'We felt that one of the wishes of the initiators was to create one organization and one building. You should be able to identify which function is where, but it should present itself as a unit. That ultimately led to this shape.'
'The zone in the middle where the escalators are looks like a lot of air, but is an efficient way to tie the floors together, making it look much more spacious.'
'We wanted to connect to the fabric of the city of Groningen, with the sequence of the squares Vismarkt, Grote Markt, Martinikerkhof, and the new market that will be located in front of the building. The stacked squares in the Forum are also a kind of market.'
'The layout of each square is different. That makes it easier to find your way.'
'To give a square character, the rooms have also been given different contours. One room you enter at the bottom and work your way up; another room you enter at the top and work your way down.'
'We also could have said: we will put all the books downstairs, and then fill the rooms. But we wanted to make that octopus, so that when you come out of the cinema you are immediately confronted with the collection. You cannot avoid that mix.'
'You have to go there to really be able to judge it.'

TYPOLOGY

THERE IS NO ARCHITECTURAL FORM
UNIQUE TO THE LIBRARY

TRANSITION;
VALUE;
TYPOLOGY;
PARTICIPATION;
INSPIRATION;
IMAGINATION;

T

WHAT ARE TYPOLOGIES AND WHY ARE THEY RELEVANT?

Lochal and Forum: two libraries that are each unique in their own way, because urban context and typology make the difference. But what exactly is a typology? Architects and art historians use typologies to identify common features or guiding principles of buildings. A typology is nothing but a classification system. It is a way of looking systematically and objectively at commonalities or resemblances between buildings.

What are the criteria, though? The most obvious option is a 'functional typology', where the specific external features of a building clearly indicate its purpose. Then it is immediately clear that it is an airport, a church, a prison, or a theatre. In addition, there are typologies that are based on social values. The building is then often an expression of the 'spirit of the times' or of a certain social ideal. It is a typology that has often been used, especially in the past, when it comes to library buildings. Virtually every historical study of library architecture mentions the Deuxième projet pour la Bibliothèque du Roi[1] (1785) designed by the French architect Étienne Louis Boullée (1728-1799), for which he was inspired by the ideas of the Enlightenment. At least as well-known is Thomas Jefferson's Rotunda[2], which symbolizes the separation of education and religion. Also well worth mentioning is the Boston Public Library from 1895, by Charles Follen McKim (1847-1909). The building is partly inspired by the Palazzo della Cancelleria in Rome.

1 https://fr.wikipedia.org/wiki/Bibliothèque_nationale_de_France (accessed August 9 2021)

2 https://en.wikipedia.org/wiki/The_Rotunda_(University_of_Virginia) (accessed August 9 2021)

'Free to All' is chiselled above the entrance, with the head of Minerva, the Roman goddess of wisdom, underneath[3]. McKim called his building a 'palace for the people', a term that American industrialist and philanthropist Andrew Carnegie also used for the hundreds of libraries he built around the beginning of the twentieth century, mostly in a classicist style[4]. A century later, Dutch architect Francine Houben also called her new public library in Birmingham (2013) a People's Palace. The outer façade of that building is a reference to the city's industrial past, and in the middle of the building there is a classical rotunda.[5]

Recognizing and using typologies can give direction in the design process of a new library building. It is a way of 'reading' and understanding existing library buildings; it provides references and ideas. You might expect that librarians—who you would think have a predilection for order and systematics—would be partial to the use of typologies when it comes to designing a new library. This does not appear to be the case, however. The use of typologies seems to belong mainly to the domain and vocabulary of architects. Librarians are missing out in this respect, as the use of typologies can be an important tool in the design process, and in the dialogue between librarian and architect.

3 https://www.bpl.org/mckim-points-of-interest/ (accessed August 9 2021)

4 Eric Klinenberg, Palaces for the people: a plea for social infrastructure as a means to fight inequality, polarization, and the decline of civic life (New York: Crown, 2018) p 24.

5 Francine Houben, People Place Purpose (London: Artifice Books on Architecture, 2015) p 197 - 245.

How to rea
library bui

WHAT DOES IT MEAN FOR PUBLIC LIBRARIES?
Are there also specific typologies of library buildings? As far as Michel Melot - former director of the Bibliothèque Nationale de France (1981-1983) and Bibliothèque Publique d'Information du Centre Georges-Pompidou (1983-1989) - is concerned, this is not the case: 'In fact, there is no architectural form unique to the library. You could say that there is no preconceived architecture for libraries like you can have for stations or stadiums.'[6]

But in 2010, Rick ten Doeschate - one of the architects of the successful LocHal - expressed a completely different opinion: 'Name me one urban building that does something similar to what a library does. There are none. So it is indeed a very important function, and thus the architectural type of that function does in fact help to determine the library'.[7] This is also in line with what Nikolaus Pevsner writes in A History of Building Types[8], the standard book on architectural typologies. In a chapter, entirely devoted to libraries, he shows how ever-changing functional and spatial requirements for library buildings resulted in a new typology.

Library buildings continuously respond to change, such as the growing size of the collection, the introduction of new media, the way those media are stored, lent, or secured, and the way users can access and use those media.[9]

6 Michel Melot, La sagesse du bibliothécaire (Paris: L'oeil Neuf, 2007)

7 Interview with CIVIC Architects Gert Kwekkeboom and Rick ten Doeschate Bibliotheekblad (1) 2019, p 38-43.

8 N.Pevsner, A History of Building Types (Princeton: The University Press, 1997)

9 U. Barbieri U, L. van Duin, M. Lampe, Plandocumentatie Bibliotheken (Delft: Publikatieburo Faculteit Bouwkunde, 1997) p 12.

d a

ding?

It is no longer about the appearance of a building—its stylistic features, the movement in which it fits or its immediate recognizability—but about how the library functions on the inside. It is a typology that deals with the purpose of different spaces and how they relate to each other. In essence: what makes a building a library, and how can you characterize the ever-changing interplay between collection and user, and between users themselves.

It also fits in with a trend in which a growing number of libraries are successfully housed in historical buildings that were never built as libraries: the LocHal in Tilburg (a former train depot), Neude Utrecht (former post office), Petruskerk Vught (Roman Catholic church), Predikheren Mechelen (former monastery).

POSSIBLE TYPOLOGIES OF A PUBLIC LIBRARY
Which library do you want to be? How do you want to organize and design the interaction between user and collection? What are some examples? And what about the various elements of the classic library typology, such as the reading and study room, information and lending counters, and separate sections for displaying the fiction and non-fiction collections?

As an aid to answering these questions, we have created a specific classification of typologies. Central to this approach are the arrangement and use of the collection, and the various ways in which this is organized. For one principle that remains unchanged is unimpeded access to the collection, and the possibility for visitors to browse it and discuss it with others.

This specific typology is based on three elements:

- The physical arrangement of the collection.
- The way visitors can browse and use the collection.
- The forms of interaction that are possible between visitors.

The classification we have made and the examples we give are neither scientifically nor historically sound, nor do they pretend to be definitive or complete. Moreover, our selection has not been limited to public libraries alone, as otherwise we would miss too many relevant historical examples, and context.
But as every librarian knows, any order is by definition debatable, and different categories are not mutually exclusive. Our structure and examples are mainly intended as an invitation to look at typologies with imagination, and to play with them yourself.

Use this QR code to get more information about typologies.
Or go to: www.imaginationandparticipation.com

agora

Agora: In ancient Greece, it was the public space for social and political life; a place for ongoing debate, like the School of Athens. During the Enlightenment, it became a monumental space for collection and user.

Examples:

- School of Athens
  Raffaello Sanzio (1510)
- French National Library
  Étienne-Louis Boullée (1785)
- OBA Amsterdam, the Netherlands
  Jo Coenen (2007)
- Stadtbibliothek Stuttgart, Germany
  Eun Young Yi (2011)
- Tianjin-Binhai library, China
  MVRDV (2017)

landscape

Landscape: where all spaces and functions flow into each other and the collection is always accessible, visible, and omnipresent; it is borderless, informal and makes room for different functions that are in open connection with each other.

Examples:

- Jussieu – Two Libraries
  OMA (1992)
- Dokk1 Århus, Denmark
  Schmidt Hammer Lassen (2015)
- PuzzleThionville, France
  Dominique Coulon & Associés (2016)
- LocHal Tilburg, the Netherlands
  Civic (2019)
- Deichman library Oslo, Norway
  Lundhagem Architects (2020)

labyrinth

Labyrinth: the library that doesn't centre around the finding of a particular book, but around searching, wandering, and serendipity. Which novelist would not love it and which librarian would not secretly want it? Immortalized by Umberto Eco and Carlos Ruiz Zafón.

Examples:

- Bangalore's Sir Seshadri Iyer Memorial
  Library, India (1915)
- Survival-library | Imaginary library
  created as part of the Brabant Libraries
  2040 project (2000)
- The Uncensored Library
  World of Minecraft (2020)

Warehouse arrangement: the library that responds to the ultimate ordering of excess, where the collection is placed row by row, like in an old-fashioned card catalogue. The bookcases structure the building and sometimes—as in The London Library—they even form the load-bearing structure of the building.

Examples:

- University Library Leiden, the Netherlands (1610)
- The London Library, United Kingdom James Osborne Smith (1922)
- Boston Public Library, United States (Johnson Building) | Philip Johnson (1972)
- Cornell University's New Fine Arts Library Ithaca (NY), United States Wolfgang Tschapeller (2019)

warehouse arrangement

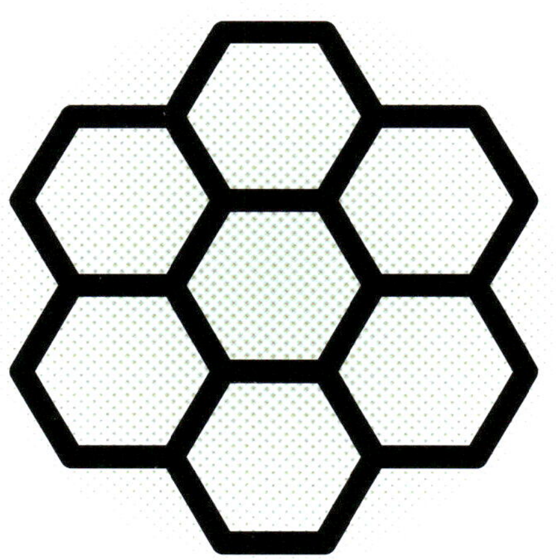

hexagon

Hexagon: who has not heard of the Library of Babel, described by librarian Jorge Luis Borges? 'The universe (which others call the Library) is composed of an indefinite, perhaps an infinite number of hexagonal galleries, with enormous ventilation shafts in the middle, encircled by very low railings. From any hexagon the upper or lower stories are visible, interminably.'

Examples:

- Atatürk Library Istanbul, Turkey Sedad Hakkı Eldem (1975)
- National Library Belarus, Republic of Belarus | Viktor Kramarenko & Mikhail Vinogradov (2006)
- Hexagone Learning Center Marseille, France | Rémy Marciano (2018)

spiral

Spiral: based on Le Corbusier's Musée à croissance illimitée and Paul Otlet's Mundaneum, and adopted by OMA, MVRDV and others. The ultimate model of a library that wants to prepare itself for an ever-growing collection. Or was Pieter Bruegel the source of inspiration?

Examples:

- Musée à croissance illimitée
  Le Corbusier (1931)
- Brabart-Library | Imaginary library created by MVRDV as part of the Brabart Libraries 2040 project.(2000)
- Seattle, Washington Public Library United States | OMA (2004)
- Musashino Art University, Tokyo, Japan Sou Fujimoto (2010)
- Book Mountain Spijkenisse, the Netherlands MVRDV (2012)

Rotunda: the circular reading room, crowned with a dome. It is a neoclassical typology, which has been used extensively from the eighteenth century to the present. It has led to many iconic libraries.
But this strict geometry was not only a source of inspiration for library buildings.

Examples:

- Oxford Radcliffe Camera, United Kingdom | James Gibbs (1749)
- The Rotunda (University of Virginia), United States | Thomas Jefferson (1826)
- Finland National Library, Helsinki, Finland | Gustaf Nyström (1906)
- Stockholm Public Library, Sweden Eric Gunnar Asplund (1928)
- Birmingham Public Library, United Kingdom | Mecanoo (2013)

rotunda

iconic

Iconic libraries: Public library buildings that are an inspiration to many architects and can be found in every architecture book, but do not directly fit into one of the categories listed here. These are completely unconventional libraries, or libraries that may yet belong to a new typology. We have limited our selection to the twenty-first century.

Examples:

- LiYuan Library, Beijing, China
  Li Xiaodong Atelier (2011)
- Culture Yard Elsinore, Denmark
  AART (2010)
- OODI Helsinki, Finland
  ALA Architects (2018)
- De Krook Ghent, Belgium
  Coussée & Goris (2017)
- Het Predikheren Mechelen, Belgium
  Korteknie Stuhlmacher Architecten (2019)

pop-up libraries

Pop-up libraries: the ultimate local library! Small-scale, semi-permanent, playful, and based on local creativity and participation. A do-it-yourself library, without many rules. This type has no typology of its own, but often has a remarkable architecture that is characterized by creativity and originality.

Examples:

- Uni Project New York, United States
  Höweler + Yoon Architecture (2013)
- Bibliothèques Sans Frontières
  Philippe Starck (2014)
- Next Library Berlin, Germany
  Raumlabor (2018)
- Catalyst Cube Caracas, Venezuela
  Will Sandy Design Studio (2019)
- Beach Library at Sharjah Beach, Dubai, United Arab Emirates
  Sharjah Beach Library Initiative (2019)

TYPOLOGIES: WHAT CAN WE LEARN FROM THEM?
Typologies look back: they show how buildings and views have changed over the years. They tell the main story of the history of library work and—thanks to distance and systematics—transcend the fads and fancies of the day. Typologies make it clear how library work itself has developed over many years, and how architecture has responded.

There is currently no single dominant old or new typology. In recently built public libraries, references to earlier typologies can however be found as part of the overall design, such as in Seattle (spiral) or Birmingham (rotunda) and Stuttgart (agora). And it is very striking that in recent decades there seems to be no causal connection between the developments related to the library building and the emergence of new media or new technologies. Library buildings are changing because their use is changing, and libraries are increasingly focused on their social mission, which is becoming broader and more multifaceted.

The history of the public library is relatively young; the first public libraries did not appear until the second half of the nineteenth century, a time of scarcity in which information was reserved for a small, privileged group in society. But thanks to philanthropic and emancipatory movements, information became accessible to all, and 'the people' could also discover the richness of the written cultural heritage.
In Bussum - one of the first public libraries built as such in the Netherlands (1914) - a stained-glass panel above the entrance to the children's department featured the text 'Eer schept ge water met een zeef—dan wijsheid zonder boeken'.[1] ('Scooping water with a sieve is like wisdom without books').

In the mid-1950s, an important turning point occurred: the collections of libraries were presented in an open and preferably attractive layout and the lending function became increasingly important, especially when book production grew exponentially in the second half of the twentieth century.[2]

From the 1970s onwards, more and more functions were added to libraries, in the form of exhibition rooms, lecture halls, classrooms, and catering facilities. In doing so, libraries literally made room for new social functions, such as lifelong learning and social encounters and debate, and the recreational function became more important. From the 1990s onwards, the collection has been increasingly focused on multimedia, which has had consequences for distribution and use. The result is a much more complex design brief for the building, especially when studios and workshops made their appearance in libraries from the 2010s onwards.

The latter marks the transition from a 'passive' library, which collects, unlocks, and makes its collection accessible, to an 'active' library, in which users are invited to engage with that collection and share knowledge with each other. The emphasis is no longer primarily on the distribution of media, but on all kinds of creativity and participation. It also means that the lending function of the library is becoming less dominant. Not only are fewer and fewer physical books being lent out, but the logistics and technology of lending are also changing, and this is having a major impact on the layout of the building. For a very long time, the counter, as the pivotal point for all lending logistics, demanded a central place in every design and thus acquired an almost iconic function.

However, the introduction of self-service in libraries put an end to this. A counter (or robot) for the returning of books with the associated walking lines is no longer necessary, and distribution points can be found at several points in the building. Counters for returning and issuing books have disappeared from many libraries, or have been given a much more modest place in the building. This also applies to the information desk, where the librarian has long been the indispensable 'host' and 'interface' between the users and the collection. But that image is changing due to new search behaviour: more 'browsing', less specific searching, the rise of digital catalogues, better (front) presentation of the collection, and the availability of almost all information on the internet via smartphones and tablets.

Library users increasingly bring their own devices with them, which also means the end of the classical reading and study rooms, which are rarely present in newly built libraries (Oodi Helsinki, LocHal Tilburg, Forum Groningen, Dokk1 Århus). They have been replaced by reading and study areas, which can be found throughout the building, and by rooms for group work. In this way, elements from the classic typology disappear and new solutions become possible, which are not determined by manageability, logistics, or efficiency, but where space is literally and figuratively created for programming, social encounters and interpretation.

1 https://www.historischekringbussum.nl/index.php/bussums-historisch-tijdschrif/1590 (accessed August 9 2021)
2 https://ourworldindata.org/books (accessed August 9 2021)

HOW THE COUNTER DISAPPEARED FROM THE PUBLIC LIBRARY BUILDING.

What also seems to be disappearing is the functional and typological distinction between the 'central library' and its 'branches'. As a rule, the central office used to provide all services, and the branches had a limited offer in terms of collections and services. The ubiquity of digital media is resulting in completely different distribution networks, whereby collection, knowledge, and services are no longer managed from one central point, but are created through a 'distributed network' in which anyone can deliver to anyone. As a result, the central library and branches are increasingly converging in terms of functionality and typology. There are, of course, differences in scale between the two, and branches often have more options for responding more quickly and directly to what their environment and users demand. It is also noticeable that branches are often no longer built as 'stand-alones', but form part of larger clusters, such as shopping centres, community buildings, or cultural facilities. A happy exception to this rule is the rise of small pop-up libraries. They are small-scale, purely local, semi-permanent facilities that primarily accommodate all kinds of educational or recreational activities and provide mini-collections. They are independent, appear at unexpected places and then disappear again, and sometimes excel in original architecture.

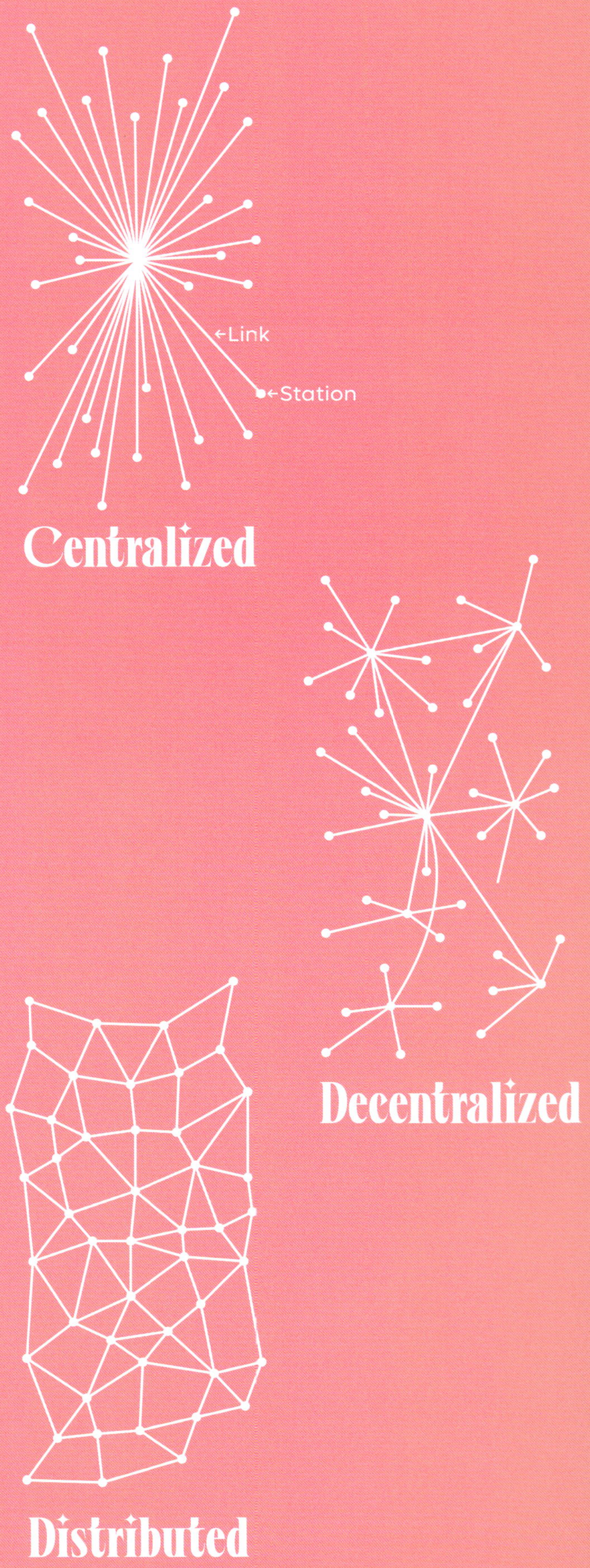

A NEW TYPOLOGY?

Is the time ripe for a new typology? And if so, what might it look like? Perhaps it is too early to answer these questions. In any case, we should be very careful with high expectations, as Stewart Brand (American writer, best known as editor of the Whole Earth Catalog) shows in his book How Buildings Learn[1]. He especially looked at the way buildings functioned after they were built: were they 'built for the future'? His conclusion is both sobering and enlightening: 'All buildings are predictions. All predictions are wrong. There is no escape from this grim syllogism, but it can be softened. Buildings can be designed and used so it doesn't matter when they're wrong.'

If everything is so uncertain, what should you plan for in the design of future libraries? The Amsterdam architects Max Cohen de Lara and David Mulder van der Vegt addressed these questions within the framework of the 'Out of the library' project, which was organized by the public libraries of Tilburg and 's-Hertogenbosch. Both libraries had plans for new buildings, and saw this as an opportunity to really respond to all the changes they were facing. They decided to have artists, designers, filmmakers, programme makers and architects travel around the world in search of original ideas for the library of the future. 'Enlarge your world, understand the world, engage with artists and become wiser' became the motto for this voyage of discovery in which Cohen de Lara and Mulder van der Vegt travelled to the west coast of the USA and visited Silicon Valley and the Seattle Public Library. Their advice is both telling and valuable: 'In this day and age, the building or renovation of a library does not require an iconographic façade architecture that envelopes a traditional interior, but a spatial strategy that responds to the accelerating development of digital technology. This architecture needs a certain oversizing, allowing the library to respond to unforeseen developments. Companies such as Google and Facebook launch new software in beta versions: a version that works but is not yet perfect, and that is further developed together with users.' This is also how they see the future of the library. Not a large, static building, but a Beta Building: '...an unstable place for ever new ways of sharing information, developing knowledge, learning and meeting each other. An environment that is both physical space and digital network. An architecture determined by programming rather than programme.' Library buildings are then no longer static and built for eternity, but become part of a permanent renewal process of public library work.
They become dynamic environments that allow for the continuous development of new forms of programming and the sharing of knowledge.

Designing the public library of tomorrow has therefore become a complex and challenging task. If librarians and architects are complementary partners in that process, it can result in a jointly developed typology. A rewarding challenge in which the librarian becomes a bit of an architect. And vice versa. The best of both worlds?

1. Stewart Brand, How Buildings learn: What happens after they're built (New York: Viking, 1994)

SOCIAL OBJECTIVES	MEANING FOR USERS	METHODOLOGY	BUILDING
PHILANTROPY (SECOND HALF 19TH CENTURY) EDIFICATION (SECOND HALF 20TH CENTURY)	ACCESSIBILITY AND GAINING KNOWLEDGE	DISTRIBUTION: MAKING AVAILABLE AND LENDING	MONO-FUNCTIONAL 'LENDING LIBRARY'
LIFELONG LEARNING (±1975 - PRESENT)	PERSONAL DEVELOPMENT, EMPOWERMENT AND LITERACY	INFORM AND TEACH	MULTI-FUNCTIONAL LIBRARY (EXHIBITIONS, LECTURES, CLASSROOMS ETC.)
LIFELONG PARTICIPATION (NEXT STEP)	COLLECTIVE INTELLIGENCE, CONTEXT AND CITIZENSHIP	ACTIVE PROGRAMMING	BETA-LIBRARY

PARTICIPATION

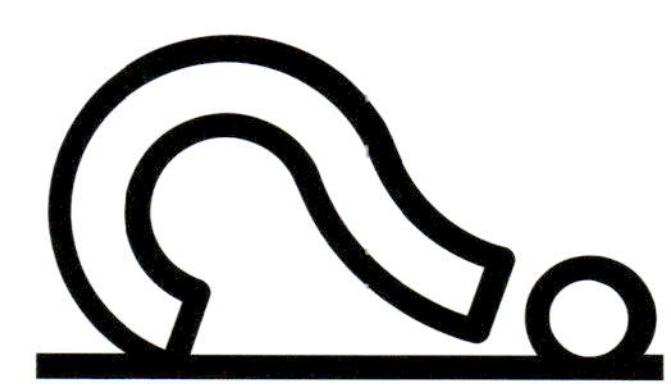

MAKING THE WORLD SAFE FOR QUESTIONS

TRANSITION:
VALUE:
TYPOLOGY:

INSPIRATION:
IMAGINATION:

THE NEW LIBRARY.

THE VALUE OF THE LIBRARY IN A SOCIAL AND URBAN CONTEXT

Years ago, we stumbled upon an article[1] in Public Libraries, the official journal of the American Library Association that is devoted to public libraries. It was written by Laurie Putnam, lecturer at the San José State University School of Information, and it immediately blew us away. This is what Laurie wrote:

'Today we need people who can help us understand complexities. We need critical thinkers, people who can see alternatives and appreciate different viewpoints. We need people who will validate their sources and ask about relevance. We need well-posed questions more than simple answers, because the answers aren't simple anymore.
Librarians can help make the world safe for questions. Our challenge, now, is to keep demonstrating our relevance, as visibly, profoundly, and convincingly as we can.
What inspiration can we offer our next generation of librarians? Simply this: that the things we do, the values we represent, and the skills we offer are critical in today's complex world.

We work in public libraries, schools, and colleges; businesses and non-profits; museums and government agencies. Every day we collect, assess, organize, and present information. But our work is really about nurturing knowledge, old and new. Wherever we work, we create places where people can tap into existing knowledge and find facts. But more importantly, we create environments where people are encouraged to ask questions and to question answers, places where people are invited to explore alternatives and find understanding, to seek answers that may lead to new questions and fresh ideas. That is what the pursuit of knowledge is all about.
In a complex world, we need people and places that preserve our ability to seek and find both questions and answers. We need people and places that can teach and inspire. Our world needs libraries and librarians, now more than ever.'

1 Laurie L. Putnam, Making the world safe for questions: why libraries and librarians are needed now more than ever. Public Libraries 44 (2) 2005, p 86-87.

Laurie wrote this in 2005, at a time when libraries were struggling to come to grips with the abundance of digital information. The predominant idea was that the existing distribution process should be adapted so that selected digital information could also be offered. Thus, efforts were still concentrated on passively presenting a collection compiled by the library, from which users could choose at their own discretion.
Apart from the fact that this would not lead to a reduction in the flood of information, it was very doubtful whether the library would be able to distinguish itself from commercial providers such as Google and Facebook. In her article, Laurie faultlessly identified the real issue by stating that making information available could no longer be the ultimate goal. Instead, it is about nurturing knowledge and insight, and creating an environment where people are encouraged to reflect upon questions and explore new perspectives.

We see this superb redefinition of the role of the library as a perfect illustration of the motto 'I have to change to stay the same'. It inspired us to design a new work process, with matching criteria for the layout of library space.

A NEW LIBRAR PROCES

Library work is still largely based on the traditional process of collection development, cataloguing, and providing access. However important this may be, it is still primarily a passive way of providing information that does not automatically lead to knowledge creation and exchange. Stimulating this requires a much more active attitude from the library, and therefore a different way of working. To put this different way of working into practice, we have designed a new process for library programming, in which the users have an important role to play. Because we are convinced that every user has something to offer, and is therefore able to make a valuable contribution to the collection and programming of the library. In other words, everyone, regardless of cultural background or educational level, is considered a member of the Scenius,[1] the community's collective intelligence. If the library adopts this attitude, every member of the community will feel welcome and valued. And that in turn means that the library can reach a greater diversity of people.

At the core of the new way of working lies the circular process of inspiration, creation and participation.
It starts by raising a topic or theme that is of importance to the local community. During an extended period of time, the library investigates this topic from a variety of angles, mobilizing all the relevant knowledge and information that is present in the community and in the library collection.
First of all, people will have to be inspired to contribute to the topic. Posing a question that arouses people's curiosity and prompts reactions can help engage them. A question to which there is no simple answer. By creating surprising collection presentations around that question, people come up with fresh ideas, and discover new aspects and points of view.
Then they are invited to actively explore the theme themselves. So, this phase is all about creating, and it can take on many forms. People can add new perspectives or connections, but also write down, draw, film, sing or even 3D print what a certain theme means to them.
If people have immersed themselves in the theme in all kinds of ways, and have thereby gained new insights or discovered new connections, they should also be able to share these with others. The next phase is therefore about participation, sharing the gained knowledge and experiences with others.
Again, this can be done in various ways, depending on what people have thought of or created. People can share these through conversations, but also through presentations or exhibitions.
Things come full circle when the results of that exchange then become part of the collection, so that people can be inspired by them again. This may actually involve new materials being added to the collection, but it may also simply be a matter of rearranging it.
And finally, the exchange can also generate a new question that people will want to explore together.
The new library process is thus a cyclical one in which each step provides valuable input for the next.

1 Scenius is a term introduced by Brian Eno. It stands for the intelligence and the intuition of a whole community. See also part 1 of the book: Transition

CONNECTION VIA COLLECTION

The collection plays an active and versatile role in the new work process. It is used as a source of knowledge and information, and as an incentive to explore new angles, but at the same time it is developing into a living archive that shows what topics have been researched and to what knowledge and insight this has led. Because of the vital role of the collection, we have come up with our own version of the much-quoted phrase 'From collection to connection'. We feel this phrase suggests that the innovation lies in shifting the focus from collecting to creating connections within the local community. We aim to create these connections through the collection itself: connection via collection. When selecting a theme, it is important to involve residents, experts, and organizations from within the local community. They are the 'connections' you need to help you think about the details of the theme, and select the sources that go with it. New resources are created through these connections, which in turn give rise to new collections and connections. So, not only is the library process cyclical, the new process of working with the collection is cyclical as well.

WHAT ARE THE CONSEQUENCES OF THE NEW PROCESS FOR THE LAYOUT OF THE BUILDING?
We see the construction of a new library or the renovation of an existing building as a unique opportunity to redefine library work. For us, it is not about creating the library of the future or a 'future-proof' library. Our motivation is to increase the quality and social relevance of library work, while maintaining the library's core values: its collection, its programming and the expertise of its staff: all must change to stay the same.

EXAMPLES OF MAKERSPACES WE RECOMMENDED FOR MUNICH'S NEW GASTEIG.

The new work process acts as a catalyst for that change. And that will inevitably have consequences for the layout of the building. So, the famous saying 'form follows function' applies here too. First of all, it means that the collection as an important source of knowledge and inspiration should be omnipresent in the building. The makerspaces also deserve a central place. After all, an important starting point is that library users and the library's partners can each contribute to the programming and the various parts of the process with their own qualities and expertise. To make their activities literally visible in the building, an open-plan design is needed, in which functions are integrated as much as possible. Makerspaces - places where people learn and create together - should therefore not be housed in a separate part of the building, but should be part of the public space. Open and accessible, so that people can see what is going on there and are more easily tempted to join in. The same principle applies to the entrance to the library. Usually, the first thing visitors see when they come into a library is an information desk. Or they find themselves in a nondescript space that is not recognizable as a library. We want them to become aware of the richness of the library immediately upon entering, so that they are encouraged to explore it.

Language and stories: the place where people work on their knowledge of the German language, or pursue their dream of writing poetry and stories themselves. German language learners are also invited to tell their stories, and then learn, together with others, how to put these stories into writing.

Youth Workshop: for children from 8 to 12 years old. Aim is to help them develop in those areas in which their talents manifest themselves most clearly. It is set up in such a way that there is something to learn, read or discover for every child.

Visual culture: where everything revolves around the transfer of culture and information through images, but where you can also draw your own manga and have it printed.

Games: for video games and board games, but also for serious gaming, and designing applications that can be used in education, healthcare or business.

Minga, the nickname given by the inhabitants of Munich to their city: examines all kinds of topics related to life in the city, such as housing, green spaces, mobility, the quality of life in the residential areas, and so on. With the help of external partners, all kinds of data are collected and visualized, so that the inhabitants of Munich can gain insight into the functioning of their city and help think of solutions to local issues.

TabulaRasa: a haven for all kinds of new experiments. Both the staff and the visitors can come up with an idea and then implement it together. The space is thus always set up on an ad hoc basis, depending on what the implementation of the idea requires.

THE BUILDING

What does this openness and fusion of functions mean for the layout of the space in concrete terms? To form an idea, we imagine the library building as a landscape. This landscape consists of a collection of diverse 'biotopes', which are connected to each other, but each with their own ambiance and appearance. There are spaces that command silence, while others stimulate liveliness and social contact; spaces where you can enjoy art, music and literature; and spaces that invite you to produce something yourself or to demonstrate your talents. The collection is arranged throughout this landscape. A pattern of paths takes you straight to your intended destination if you wish, but also allows you to wander and let yourself be surprised by what you find along the way. The landscape is thus characterized by an informal atmosphere, openness, variety, natural connections, an attractive and colourful layout, and the possibility to wander.

One of the projects in which we have used the idea of the library as a landscape is our consultancy for the Munich City Library. The library, which will undergo a major renovation in the coming years, is housed in the Gasteig, Germany's largest and most successful cultural centre, together with the Concert Hall, the College of Music and Theatre, and the Institute for Adult Education. A major challenge in the renovation of the building, which dates from 1985, was the desire to create more synergy and creative cooperation between the various partners in the building. In our vision, the landscape typology was an excellent solution, because it allowed us to create an environment that encourages participation and the free exploration of all that the partners collectively have to offer in terms of knowledge and culture.
An inspiring example of this is Le Centquatre (Le104), a unique cultural centre, located in the 19th arrondissement of Paris. In this monumental building, which once served as a mortuary, the traditional boundary between producer and consumer is blurred. Visitors are free to walk in and watch acrobats, jugglers, musicians, dancers, actors and artists at work. But what is most special is that as a visitor, you are free to join in and give a spontaneous performance yourself. So, each time you visit, you can choose which role you want to play: that of a spectator, a passer-by, a dancer, an artist, or anything else.
The qualities of Le104 - its informal and inviting character, the cross-pollination between the various cultural disciplines, and the disappearance of the boundaries between the public and the producers of information and cultural expressions - should, in our opinion, also be leading in the design of a library.

LIBRARY AS A LANDSCAPE

WHOM TO WORK WITH?

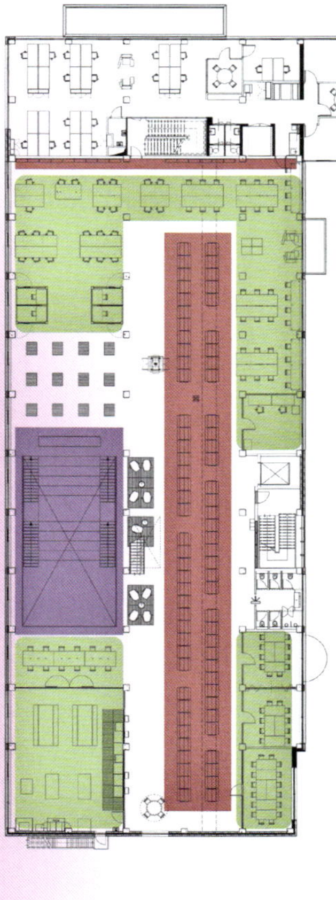

The new work process, which is based on collaboration, also sets out which parties you can and cannot work with. This may sound strange, but in order to achieve true integration in terms of space and content, it is important that the partners in the building form a unity despite their diversity. This means no parties that hole themselves up in their own part of the building, but fellow institutions in the local community that have a related mission, and on that basis can make a substantial and substantive contribution to the library's programming in harmonious cooperation, so that the whole becomes greater than the sum of its parts. Practice has taught us that three types of cooperation partners can be distinguished:

- collecting institutions, such as museums, archives, and special libraries.
- creative partners, with the know-how and facilities to help users deepen or broaden their knowledge. These may include adult education centres, creativity centres, creative education, artists, theatre makers, and storytellers.
- partners who help users to express and share the insights they have acquired. These include partners in all kinds of different makerspaces, spaces where people gather to create stories, videos, podcasts, 3D prints, and so on. Of course, the local press is also an obvious partner.

A place where the cooperation between parties is truly visible in the layout of space is the Chocolate Factory in Gouda, a Dutch town with a population of 73,000. The Chocolate Factory, which opened in 2015, was designed by the Ministry of Imagination. It houses the Public Library, the Mid-Holland Archive, The Gouda Fine Printing Society, and Restaurant Kruim. From the start it was clear that the partners really wanted to work together. They all agreed there were to be no walls between them. The aim was to create a communal space where all functions would be integrated - instantly visible and accessible to all visitors.
This shared vision allowed us to create an open plan design, based on the new work process. A source of inspiration was the history of the building, which formerly housed a real chocolate factory. By applying the process of inspiration, creation, and participation, we were able to preserve the idea of a production site; not of chocolate, but of knowledge and ideas. We regarded the collections of the library and the archive as the starting point of the inspiration process. They were the raw material, used for the production of knowledge. And just like in a real factory, we decided upon a compact storage of this raw material. In most libraries, 70 to 80 percent of space is taken up by bookcases, leaving limited space for other amenities and activities. In the Chocolate Factory it is only 30 percent. Combined with the open floor plan and integration of partners, this allowed us to create a variety of makerspaces and social spaces: the much-needed room for creation and participation. For instance, the youth workshop, inviting children to develop their different talents, the media workshop for composing multi-media productions, and the print workshop where craftsmen teach their skills.

LEGENDA

- inspiration
- creation
- participation

EXAMPLE
CHOCOLATE FACTORY NARRATIVE

EVERY BUILDING TELLS A STORY

Although the process of inspiring, creating and participating forms the basis of all our designs, the result is never the same. This is because we always take inspiration from the local context: the significance of the library for the local community, the location, and the character and history of the building, if it concerns an existing building. After thorough research into these aspects, we, together with management and staff, create an authentic 'narrative' of the library, a clear and appealing story describing the main drivers of the organization, and how these will be expressed in the design of the building. The narrative helps to avoid uniformity, and provides each library with a strong, distinctive identity.

The Chocolate Factory in Gouda is housed in the old factory building of Steenland Chocolate B.V. The company, which is still based in Gouda, grew from a manufacturer of traditional Dutch products to an international exporter. Thousands of litres of liquid chocolate flowed through the place when it was a factory, eventually to be distributed all over the world in the form of nicely packaged chocolate figurines, cigarettes and coins.

To preserve the idea of a factory, we used industrial-style materials throughout the building. Books, for example, are being displayed on stacks of wooden pallets and sea containers serve as silent study cubicles.
We also placed the self-service units for borrowing and returning books in the factory's former loading and unloading area. But to emphasize the history of the building even more, designer Florian de Visser came up with a brilliant idea. He explored the archives, spoke with the company's former director, and then drew a unique floor design in which you can see the layout of the old chocolate factory. The production process, the machinery that stood here, the stories of the people who worked here: all of this is now visible in the new Chocolate Factory.

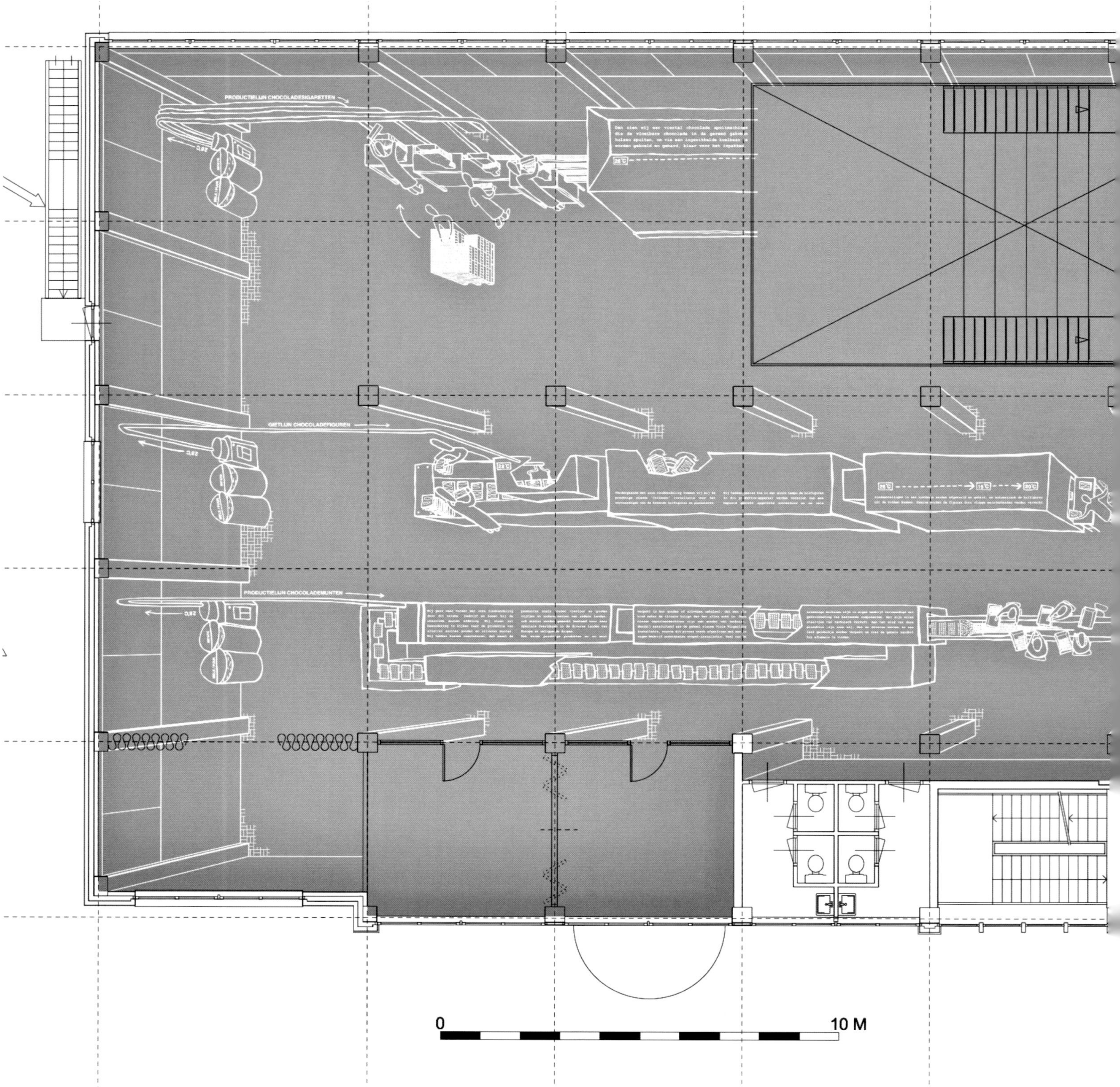
PRODUCTIELIJN CHOCOLADESIGARETTEN
GIETLIJN CHOCOLADEFIGUREN
PRODUCTIELIJN CHOCOLADEMUNTEN
0
10 M

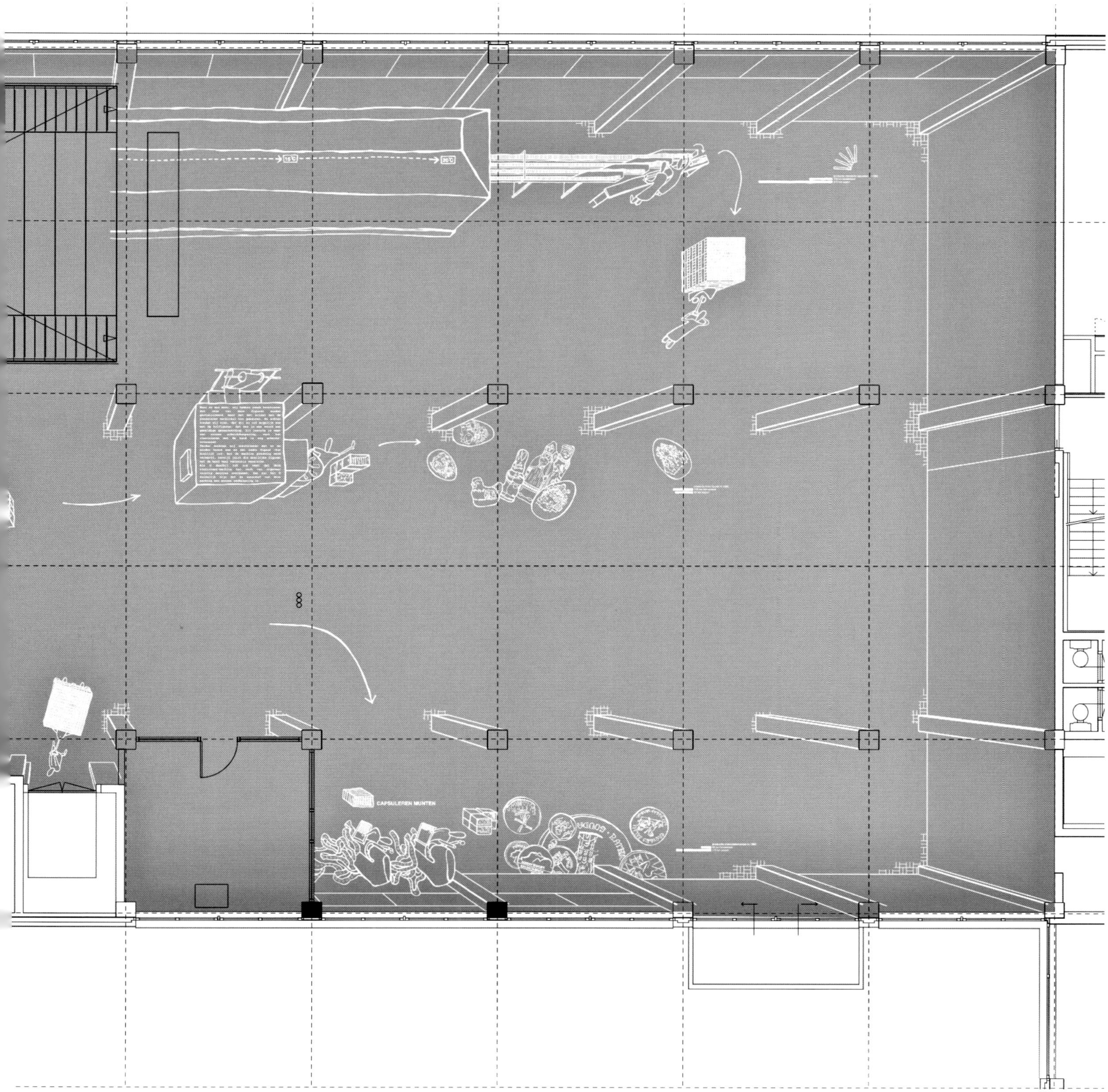

15°C
20°C
CAPSULEREN MUNTEN

EXAMPLE
CULTURE STATION NARRATIVE

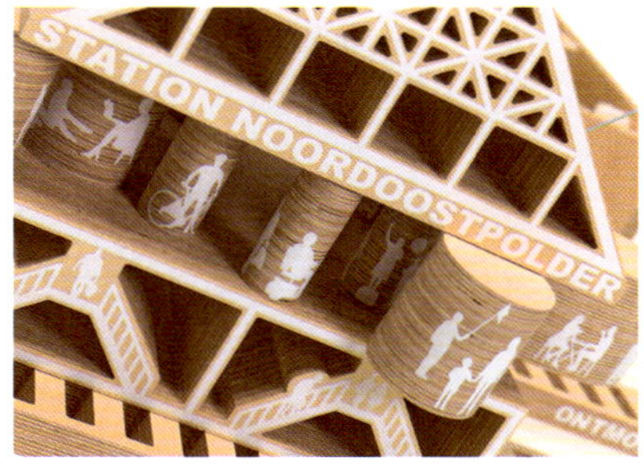

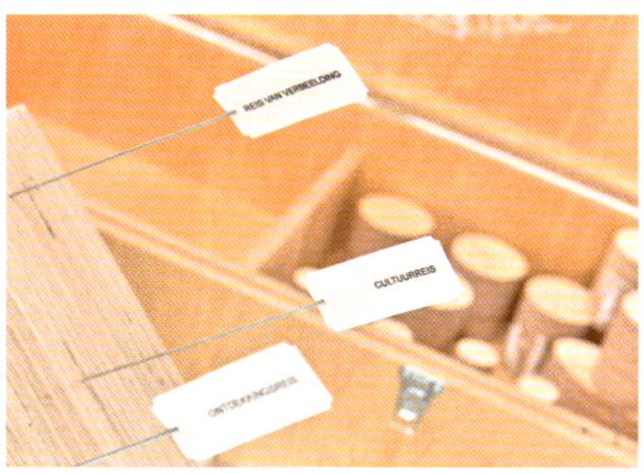

A narrative also allows you to explain in an appealing way—and without using policy language—what your library stands for, and what you aspire to achieve with the new building. An example is the narrative of the Culture Station in the Dutch town of Emmeloord.
Here, the library, together with the regional organization for art, culture, and heritage, would like to create a joint cultural facility that breaks down the traditional boundary between providers and recipients of information and culture. The metaphor of the station was chosen to highlight how people can go on a journey through the rich programmes of both institutions, and easily switch over when they discover something they didn't come for in the first place. They can also choose the role they want to play: that of passer-by, spectator, traveller, reader, storyteller, expert, musician, or exhibitor. In addition, the metaphor of the station also wryly refers to a frustration of the people of Emmeloord, namely that there is no railway line leading to their town, and therefore no train station.
In order to express the ambitions for the new building in an attractive, visual manner, Florian de Visser depicted the Culture Station as a travelling storytelling theatre. This was a conversation piece in itself, but to make the story even more imaginative, a toolbox of storytelling plates depicting different journeys was added. Loosely inspired by the Japanese kamishibai, which literally translates as 'paper theatre', the journeys were illustrated by means of performances that could be shown one by one in a box. The story of the partnership could thus be told in different places and to different audiences, and the toolbox could easily be supplemented if new ideas or ingredients for journeys came up.

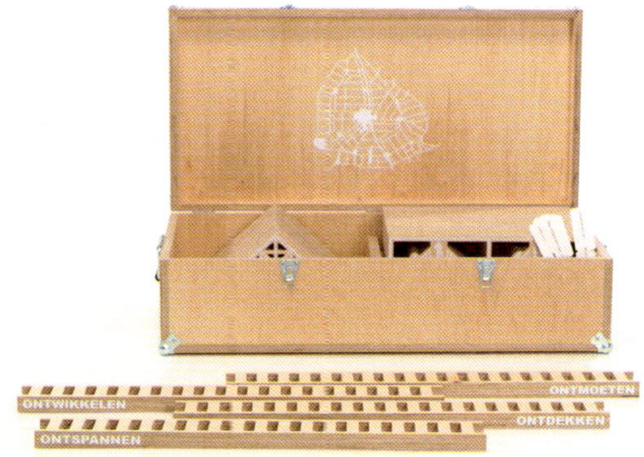
ONTMOETEN
ONTWIKKELEN
ONTDEKKEN
ONTSPANNEN

ONTMOETEN
ONTWIKKELEN
ONTDEKKEN
ONTSPANNEN

ONTMOETEN
ONTWIKKELEN
ONTDEKKEN
ONTSPANNEN

ONTWIKKELEN
ONTMOETEN
ONTDEKKEN
ONTSPANNEN

ONTWIKKELEN
ONTMOETEN
ONTDEKKEN
ONTSPANNEN

MANIFESTO OF THE MINISTRY OF IMAGINATION

The new work process means that we have become much more aware of how users will experience the future building. After all, we want as many people as possible to visit the library, and be able to identify with what goes on inside. Therefore, we need to have an idea of the different ways they will perceive the building. What would they expect to find there, and how can we inspire them and invite them to actively participate, even those who do not normally come into contact with art and culture? And how do we ensure that the appearance, atmosphere, and furnishings match the various reasons people have for visiting the library?

To have a clearer idea of this, we have taken the future users in mind and expressed their positive impressions and experiences in a number of statements. The inspiration for this initially came from Nina Simon, who in her book The Participatory Museum[1] lists five commonly-expressed forms of public dissatisfaction that people experience when visiting a museum. We converted those comments into positive statements, and then refined them to apply to library visitors. Together, they form the Manifesto of the Ministry of Imagination, an ideal image of the future library, which we are trying to emulate as best we can.

1 Nina Simon, The Participatory Museum (Santa Cruz, Calif: Museum 2.0, 2010) Available online at: http://www.participatorymuseum.org/read/ (accessed August 11 2021)

MANIFESTO

All public libraries face the same challenge: they need to rethink and rework their spaces and their strategies to promote deeper understanding, by active use of their collections, greater interactivity, and a more meaningful range of activities. To illustrate this the Ministry has drawn up five positive comments about the library you would be happy to hear from your visitors. They refer to various forms of interaction and co-creation that will help increase active engagement and add new meaning to the collection.

'The library is of importance in my life.'

If the library adopts an inquiring attitude and responds actively to ideas, stories, and creative work offered by visitors, people will feel that their contribution matters, regardless of their social or cultural background or their educational level.

'I keep coming back because there's always something new to experience.'

By bringing visitors into contact with interesting questions and new ideas and by enabling them to share knowledge, stories and skills amongst each other, the library offers constantly changing experiences.

'It provides me with the necessary context to understand issues and developments and leaves room for new interpretations.'

By presenting multiple viewpoints on themes and issues that concern the local community, the library helps visitors to reflect upon their own opinions and stimulates them to understand different perspectives.

'It's a creative place where I can express myself and contribute to the collection.'

By inviting visitors to participate, the library supports the interests of those who prefer to make and do rather than just use the collection in a passive way. These different expressions provide a new context that enriches the collection.

'It's a comfortable social place for me to talk about ideas with friends and strangers.'

By designing opportunities for interpersonal dialogue, the library distinguishes itself as a trusted and desirable location for discussion about important issues related to the content presented.

INSPIRATION

CONVERSATIONS with ARCHITECTS

I

RALF COUSSÉE

A conversation with

'We always want to make a lyrical building, a poetic building'

COUSSEE GORIS
HUYGHE ARCHITECTS

KLAAS GORIS

The making of a room, as Louis Kahn describes it, is about creating a place where you want to spend time.’

Ralf Coussée & Klaas Goris

We cross the border

to Flanders to talk to Ralf Coussée and Klaas Goris of COUSSEE GORIS HUYGHE architects[1]. Together with the Spanish architecture firm RCR Arquitectes[2], COUSSEE & GORIS architects are responsible for the design of De Krook, the new city library of Ghent, Belgium, which opened in 2017 and houses, among other organizations, Imec (a research centre for nanoelectronics and digital technology), and Ghent University. As the only non-Dutch architects in the series, they should not be missing from the list, because we think that with De Krook they have constructed an iconic building. A concept that is open to multiple interpretations, as the conversation shows.

1 https://coussee-goris-huyghe.com
2 https://www.rcrarquitectes.es

THE DESIGN BRIEF FOR THE LIBRARY DATED BACK TO 2009 AND WAS WRITTEN BY DIRECTOR LUC BAUWENS, WHO RETIRED IN 2011. DID THAT COMPLICATE THINGS FOR YOU?
'In the competition design, you create an image from the specifications that Luc has written, but you have no means of communicating about it. Of course, afterwards we talked about the things that we had understood differently from what he had intended, but from experience we had already approached it a little more intelligently. We accepted the commission on the condition that we could make programme modifications, and we had two or three days to make them. It was about shifting surfaces. Our building was designed in such a way that the size of all the plateaus could still be increased or decreased during the construction phase. So, we could just create some additional square metres if needed, and this immediately was the case. When you are dealing with five partners in a building, you cannot expect them to immediately agree on everything. Because we were able to play with these plateaus, it was possible to take functions that were initially conceived at level minus two up to level four. This allowed us to make changes, while the building still retained the same language.

It is a huge building for Ghent, 18,000 square metres. Playing with those plateaus was a deliberate choice to make the project less massive, to let the light fluctuate through it. It would otherwise have become too heavy in the urban landscape. Afterwards, someone made a caricature of the building: a stack of books of different sizes. But this was not a conceptual idea of ours. That is more something you may expect from someone from the Netherlands, because they are much more image-oriented. That is not the way we work.'

THIS MAKES US CURIOUS ABOUT THE DIFFERENCE BETWEEN DUTCH AND FLEMISH ARCHITECTS.
'We still manage our construction sites ourselves, so we see how something is built, that is the main difference. In the case of De Krook, it involved all kinds of prefabricated metal elements. 85 percent of all these materials were transported to the construction site by water. If all of that had to be transported in lorries, it would have turned the city upside down. We included that in our plans from the start. You can create some flashy image of a building, but at the end of the day, it is the construction that is at the heart of it.

We also analyse the environment very thoroughly. What are elements that we can work with? This is how we came up with the urban oasis, the idea of creating an oasis by the water. To attract many people to your building, the landscape around it needs to be attractive. So, that is one thing. We made the urban connection by creating two levels. In addition to the library, we also made a master plan for the nearby Winter Circus. The Winter Circus was supposed to house a spin-off from the university that was all about digital developments. The idea was to have the Winter Circus and the library write a story together. But between the entrance to the Winter Circus and the ground level of the water at the Waalse Krook there is almost an 8-metre difference. So, we thought: let's raise the entrance to the library by one floor, then you only have one level difference. The interesting thing is that as a result, the level from South, as we call it, is now more connected to the part of the city you want to go to. So, the design of that urban connection was created through two systems: a fast connection at the entrance level and a slow connection to the city, to the water, and to the neighbourhood below. This is a calm connection because the people around the building are not disturbed by it.

This urban connection is also the essential difference with the other projects. Architect Toyo Ito, for example, had designed a building for the site, and afterwards a small bridge would be built somewhere, but without that link to the surroundings. In Ghent, people never knew what to do with that site; it was always just there, in a state of disrepair. So, we thought it was our job to first think about the question: how can we get this place out of the doldrums, and plant our building there? That place is called the Waalse Krook because there is a bend in the river Scheldt, a 'fold'. Ships from Wallonia came through it with coal or bluestone from the Tournai region for the construction of churches. We wanted to follow that bend, and thus put a fold in our building. The main reason is that we wanted to make the volume look less heavy, just like we did with those staggered plateaus.
Because whether you come from one side or the other, you never immediately see the building in its entirety, which makes it seem less massive.

'The making of a room, as Louis Kahn describes it, is about creating a place where you want to spend time.'

Another important element of our project is the 'city within the city'. The making of a room, as Louis Kahn describes it, is about creating a place where you want to spend time. How can you realize that, how do you turn it into a living room for the city? Our entire building is actually a balcony over the city and the river. We even had the idea of making these balconies accessible, but that was rejected for safety reasons. By making huge cut-outs inside, we also created a balcony over the agora and the interior, so that you can look down on the building from there. We always want to make a lyrical building, a poetic building. It is not just about functionality, it is also about well-being, about light and acoustics. It should not look like an office building. We always want to transcend that. It has to be much more lyrical.

These are the elements with which we build such a project. And that goes beyond just painting a pretty picture. We try to describe what experiences you want visitors to have there, how to make them all feel at home, how to make it a success story. And it has been a success: the library anticipated that there would be 4,000 visitors a day, and we are now at 7 to 8,000.

> 'We prefer to look at what the building has done after a year. How many people have enjoyed it and have been brought together by it.'

As for painting pictures, politicians always want a pretty picture too. People said about our design that it was not an iconic building. We prefer to look at what the building has done after a year. How many people have enjoyed it and have been brought together by it. If a building has such an impact, it is not so much about whether it is iconic. In the end it did become an icon, because quite a few cartoonists have used it in their drawings. And in the television reports of the recent municipal elections, De Krook was shown alongside images of Mechelen, Brussels, and Antwerp. So, it has become an important landmark for Ghent.'

GHENT NOW HAS TWO ICONIC LIBRARIES. THE BOEKENTOREN ('BOOK TOWER'), THE UNIVERSITY LIBRARY, WHICH TOWERS OVER THE CITY, AND DE KROOK, WHICH HAS MUCH MORE OF A HORIZONTAL APPEARANCE. WAS THAT YOUR INTENTION?

'Yes, very much so. If you look at the roofs in Ghent, you can see that we have stayed within the line of those roofs. The Book Tower [by architect Henry Van der Velden] towers above it, just like the cathedral. We are very focused on maintaining the appearance of the Flemish city, as it is in Holland: a horizontal line with some peaks. Think of Vermeer's View of Delft, for example. We are very critical of high-rise buildings, although we will soon be working on the Belgacom tower [50 metres high, also called the ugliest building in Ghent], but that is because it is already there. Those high towers are not always very connected to the city, are they? From a social point of view, we are quite critical of this. We always say: about four or five layers, then you are still in contact with the street, but above that, the city becomes a map. In the Netherlands, there is much more of a tendency to build tall buildings. In Flanders, you have architects who are more Romanesque, like us, but you also have many who come from the Dutch sphere of influence. And they all promote towers. We are very weary of this, and always have the impression that they do so more from a speculative point of view—because it has to make a lot of money—than that there is a vision of society behind it. But an architect should have such a vision.

Ghent is not a medieval city, but what is medieval is the unbuilt space, the air between the buildings. The streets, the squares, and how you meander through them. That is something we always include in our projects. The location of our building will define the space around it. It is very important for us to think about what that means. Because it is a way of anchoring a building in the landscape, be it urban or rural. When architects study a city, they make a Nolli plan. Giambastista Nolli was an Italian who made an inverted map, in which the buildings were black, and the unbuilt space was white. It is very interesting to study a city in that way. We always assess what the influence of a building will be on its surroundings.'

HOW CAN WE RECOGNIZE YOUR BUILDINGS?

'It's not always the appearance that is interesting, but rather the whole process. You can just look at De Krook as a building, but for us it is also an urban development project. Maybe that's why it takes a little more time to discover it. That only later people will say: this is not how we understood it, but this is how we have come to feel about it.
We do not think of ourselves as inventors; we are real ruminants. That is, we did a project, and in the next project we will analyse what has happened in it. We build on this, and make innovations. You can see this in many of our projects. We think along different tracks, so there are different approaches. Although our projects are very diverse, they are all related to each other. If you look at the youth and recreation domain De Boerekreek, which we had the honour of building in Sint-Jan-in-Eremo, you can see that the visitors' centre at Het Zwin is actually its brother. We have built a glass skin around a department store in Rumbeke, and are now restoring a former power station, placing a kind of bell jar around the building. That is a theme of ours, but we always go deeper into it. Because it is actually about how to build a shell, because that is what a building is, around a collection of people. And this can be done with different materials and from different points of view. Koen Van Synghel, who wrote a book about us, compared our work to a Russian matryoshka. You have a doll, and there is another doll in it, and then another.

By ruminating we mean that we rely heavily on our own experiences. With building, with the people who build it, with politics, but also financially. With how you can build something quickly, but also, for example, how you can save on what we call 'frillaria'. Our buildings are always a kind of glorified

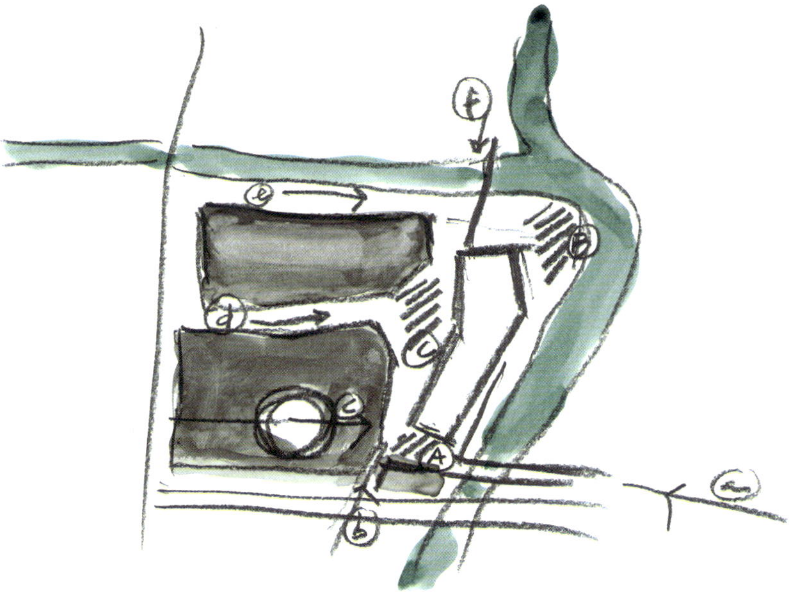

building shell. With us, the construction phase is also the finishing phase. That is also a philosophy that is part of our work. You shouldn't paint in a library. At most, you have to change the carpet, or replace a tile. When we started, we often thought that it had become such a strong building. As soon as they started finishing, that disappeared. And so did the magic. From these experiences we have learned that we should construct a building as a kind of shell. Our architecture is therefore closely related to the building's authenticity. Our engineer, with whom we have been working for years, really understands this too. You reduce it to its essence, so it doesn't have to be painted every other year, costing you a fortune.

The less finishing you do in your building, the stronger that building can hold its own against all the elements you bring into it. We are not decorators; we are constructors. So, a building like De Krook is like a child assembling Meccano [a toy erector set]. And it could become a shopping mall or something else next week. We are not building it to look like a library; we are building it to look like a public building.'

YOU'VE BEEN KNOWN TO SAY THAT LIBRARIES ARE A BIT OF A MESS, AND THEREFORE NEED A CLEAR STRUCTURE.

'The competition's brief stated that the building was not to have columns. But the first thing we proposed when we were selected for the project was to put in 700 columns. Our story was that a column is a structure that also has a structuring effect in space. They indicate zones. This is what we call point de repère in French, a kind of reference point to base your interior on. Hence, these columns are a huge presence in the library. They structured the space that could then be filled according to the requirements. This made everything fit together.
And there were other ideas that we abandoned, such as the large reading room. Initially, we had imagined three levels, connected by a staircase, and with three large bookcases in it. After we won the competition and talked to Luc Bauwens, he said he would prefer those bookcases to be spread around the building, so that he could create different spaces. We ourselves were also in favour of doing things differently, but in a competition like this you always need certain images for the politicians, don't you? They already thought our building was not iconic, so the image of that space with those high bookcases was very important. But it is a good thing we didn't go through with it. Luc thought: there will be a murmur there, and I want the library to gradually become quiet. And it worked, because the higher you go, the quieter it gets.'

WE ARE VERY INTERESTED IN THIS SUBJECT, BECAUSE WHAT IS IT EXACTLY THAT MAKES PEOPLE GO QUIET WHEN THEY ENTER A CERTAIN SPACE?

'We attach great importance to acoustics. The ceiling is a so-called cooling ceiling that consists of slats, which provide acoustic absorption. We have received much praise for the acoustics, especially from the staff. Because it actually starts with that, doesn't it? If you don't have silence in a library, it is hard to read a book there. On a related note, one of the criticisms we sometimes receive about our library is that it is dark. Measurements show that there is actually plenty of light. But there is a reason why it seems dark. If you want to create a balcony overlooking the city and the interior is too light, you won't be able to see the city. The city is illuminated by the fact that you darken the space. The darkness also has an enormous effect in terms of silence. That is something that is underestimated. When you enter a dark room, you tend to speak more softly, to whisper. It probably has something to do with day and night. At night you are quieter than during the day. Beautiful things have been said about this by Jun'ichirō Tanizaki in his book In Praise of Shadows. About the power of the darkness to evidence the light. We used that. One of Le Corbusier's bold statements is: light is not very tangible, but shade is much more tangible, so shade is evidence of the power of light.

We have also applied this in Crematorium Hofheide. We did not want any artificial light there, so that you fall silent when you come in from a very beautiful landscape. We were inspired by Romanesque churches in this respect.'

> ‘The library is currently the most public building you can make.’

WOULD YOU LIKE TO DESIGN ANOTHER LIBRARY?
‘We asked ourselves the same question with regard to the crematorium. Then we said no, because we have done something there that we could never top. The situation is different for the library. It is a less hermetic programme, because every location is different. Libraries are increasingly expected to be social condensers [places where boundaries between population groups are bridged, and social equality is promoted]. That’s why we’re so interested in them. It is currently the most public building you can make. An incredible diversity of people come there, and the threshold is very low, or at least it should be. The Waalse Krook was a fantastic site for a library, near the water and very central to the city. It would even have been a shame to build something else in that unique place. In that sense, we think we would like to try another library.’

FRAN

A conversation with

'A good library has character

CINE HOUBEN

MECANOO

and is not dogmatic'

'I start by getting to know the city, its people, history and future. I also try to understand the collection.'

Francine Houben

It is safe to say that the renewed

interest in public library buildings is in no small part due to Francine Houben, founder and creative director of Mecanoo[1] architects. She gained international fame with her design for Birmingham UK library, the building with the distinctive filigree pattern of metal circles on the façade, a reference to Birmingham's history as a jewellery city, and centre of the British iron and steel industry.

1 https://www.mecanoo.nl

Mecanoo was also responsible for the interior design of Tilburg's LocHal, a much-awarded public library in the Netherlands. When we spoke with her, Francine was still busy with the Tainan Public Library in Taiwan and the renovation of the Martin Luther King Library in Washington, both completed in 2020, and the Stavros Niarchos Foundation Library in New York, completed in 2021. An equally prestigious project, that is scheduled to be completed in 2023, is the renovation of The New York Public Library Stephen A. Schwarzman Building, the famous building with the lions. But the architectural firm is certainly not only involved in the design and renovation of large libraries. They have, for example, had the pleasure of working on the renovation of a library on Mercatorplein in Amsterdam, a branch of the Amsterdam Public Library.

WHERE DO YOU BEGIN WHEN DESIGNING A LIBRARY?
'I myself start by getting to know the city, its people, history and future. I also try to understand the collection. I didn't do that with my very first libraries, but in Birmingham I learned how important that is, so in Washington – and certainly in New York – I wanted to study the collection. It seems to me that many architects have come to regard books almost as a kind of decoration, whereas it is very much about what the collection is, and what you want to do with it. Children's books, a collection on the history of the city, they all deserve their own place. The bottom line is that I always try to understand what a library wants to offer, what it wants to achieve. And that is different every time. But the main challenge is perhaps: making the building suitable for all different target groups. I learned that in the UK and America: it's for everybody. Everyone is welcome, and one group should not drive out another. I have become very principled about this, but in the Netherlands, I don't really feel that libraries are there for everyone.'

'I start by getting to know the city, its people, history and future. I also try to understand the collection.'

The conversation briefly turns to the issue of paid membership. Francine thinks the library ought to be free. This is the case in almost all other countries, but not in the Netherlands. She sees it as a necessary economic and cultural investment in people, and thinks that Dutch politicians are not sufficiently aware of this. 'It is so important that libraries are there for all people. In the past, many libraries were designed to impress. These gave the impression that you had to be very intelligent to use them. We must leave this typology behind us, especially with public libraries. They have to be as accessible as possible and there is no standard solution for that, because there is no such thing as one universal library.'

IN THE NETHERLANDS, THOUGH, FOR A LONG TIME, THE TENDENCY WAS TO STRIVE FOR UNIFORMITY OF LIBRARIES.

'Yes, but that turned out to be naive. I am sure it was done with good intentions, but what you have to provide in the OBA Oosterdok [central library] in Amsterdam is something completely different from what you have to provide in a neighbourhood library in Amsterdam West. Cities such as Rotterdam and Amsterdam are already very different, in population, in culture. The fact that you have to do justice to those differences is something I really learned when I worked on the library of Birmingham.'

New York Public Library
New York Public Library
Library
Library

'Our motto is: design for predictable and unpredictable change.'

IS THAT ALSO CHARACTERISTIC OF MECANOO? THAT YOU COULD ONLY BUILD THE LIBRARY OF BIRMINGHAM IN THAT CITY?
'Yes, you could perhaps say so. I wanted to design a library that is truly for Birmingham. There are themes in it that are universal, but for me it literally developed from observing and playing in my head with what I found out about the city. Other architects sometimes have their own architectural language, and build a library on that basis. That is also a way to do it, but it's not how my colleagues and I work. The out-come is different everywhere, because you always take the surroundings, the context, into account. And change, of course. Our motto is: design for predictable and unpredictable change.'

WHAT IS THE COOPERATION WITH THE LIBRARY LIKE IN THAT DESIGN PROCESS?
'That's the beauty of it: we bring knowledge and experience from other countries and cities and they bring theirs too, so we really are partners in dialogue. We also listen very carefully to the people of the library and learn what the specific problems of the city are. It is interesting, for example, to discover how all these different cities approach young people; it is always difficult to make the library attractive for them. I was in Boston recently, and they have created a huge library for teenagers that is packed at certain times. Then I go and talk to the librarians: what works and what doesn't? You then learn that it is virtually empty during school hours and holidays and that the youngsters use the library as a stop-over before going home.'

'Library people are not trained to design a building, but if they dare to think ahead, into the future, you're halfway there. The question is: what do they want to change and what do they want to hold on to?'

SO YOU ALWAYS MANAGE TO MAKE THINGS WORK WITH THE LIBRARY?

'Yes, we contribute our knowledge, but of course it is the library that decides. They determine the programming and that is what a library is all about. Library people are not trained to design a building, but if they dare to think ahead, into the future, you're halfway there. The question is: what do they want to change and what do they want to hold on to? Architects sometimes fail because they do not fully understand what a library essentially is. When I teach at Yale [Francine is a visiting professor at the Yale School of Architecture in New Haven, Connecticut USA] I try to explain this to the students. They often start with the game of 'where do we put all the books' and 'where can we create some nice spaces', while it is all about the right combinations. A library in Manhattan's Chinatown requires several rooms, each with its own purpose and collection. A room for the Chinese collection, the English collection, a department for Chinese people who want to start their own business, and a room for the children who are allowed to come there without parents because they are always at work. That game of figuring out how it should all fall into place is something I really enjoy.'

IN NEW YORK, YOU ARE RENOVATING AN EXISTING BUILDING, THE STAVROS NIARCHOS FOUNDATION LIBRARY. DOES THAT ALSO COME DOWN TO THE QUESTION OF WHAT SHOULD BE CHANGED AND WHAT YOU WANT TO HOLD ON TO?

'Yes, and that is not easy sometimes. It is a "circulating library" where they work with "floating collections", so the library basically has the collection the visitors ask for. We have a loyal group of users there who want 400,000 books to remain available, exactly the same number as in the past. The challenge is to give those books a place while simultaneously creating space for all the target groups that visit the library: children, young people, adults and yes, also the homeless, which is a recurring theme in the US.'

WHAT DO YOU THINK DEFINES A GOOD PUBLIC LIBRARY?

'A good library has character and is not dogmatic. Libraries nowadays are very preoccupied with the interior, and tend to play around with books or opt for curved shelves instead of straight ones. Others may do so, but I don't like it. I have learned to work with sight lines and they are often lost in such constructions. For me, the library is an institution.
It should be inviting. And straight rows of cabinets and long tables are part of that. In that respect, I find it very interesting to work on the Martin Luther King Library in Washington, because of the incredibly long sightlines in that building. I also always think about the circulation in a building. I want people to be able to take a journey through the building.'

COULD YOU GIVE US SOME EXAMPLES THAT HAVE INSPIRED YOU?

'Then I think of classics, such as the Asplund Library in Stockholm, Sweden. And I am still proud of the library of the University of Technology in Delft, the Netherlands [completed in 1998], because it really has character. When you walk in, you immediately know that you are in a library, but there is still that welcoming atmosphere. Actually, I am thinking of all kinds of different images from places and libraries. There are good libraries in the Netherlands, but I don't have a clear favourite. Dutch libraries are quite progressive in a number of areas, but it would be arrogant to think that they are ahead in all respects. In other countries, libraries are often much more part of the DNA of society.
They are real community places, and that is less the case in the Netherlands.'

Literary Collections

A conversation with

JO COE

'This is the way,

OBA

NEN

no doubts, Jo.'

‘I don’t believe I have to go along with every ripple.’

Jo Coenen

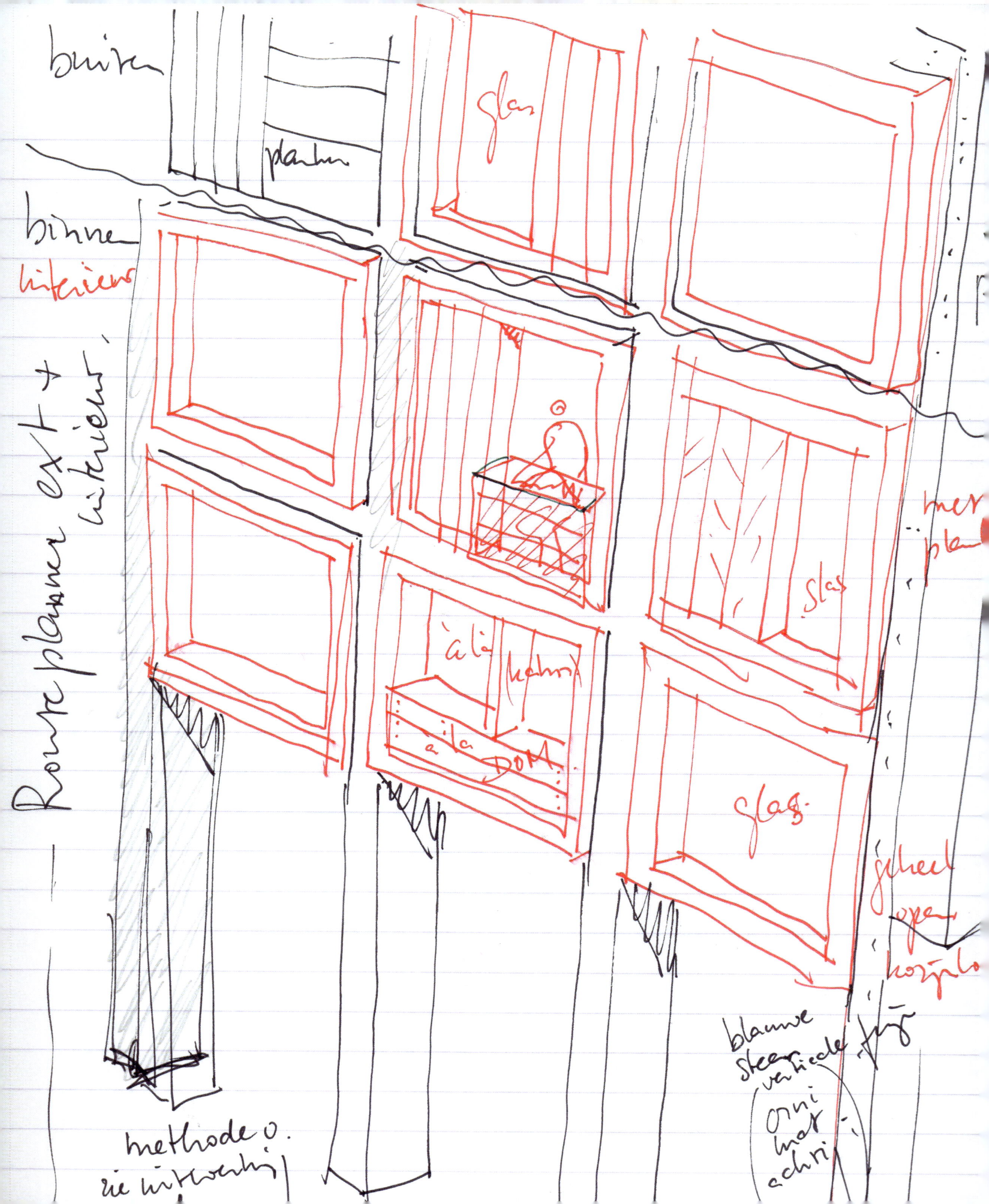

buiten
planken
binnen
glas
à la
glas
glas
methode

07-07-07

a date

that is etched in the memory of architect Jo Coenen[1]. And not just in his, but in that of countless library staff. Because on that day the Amsterdam Public Library (OBA), designed by Jo, opened its doors, a new prestigious library that gave the library sector renewed confidence in the future. Earlier, Jo Coenen had also designed the Centre Céramique in Maastricht (NL), a building realized in 1999 that houses the city library and the municipal archives. These are just a few examples from his extensive oeuvre and successful international career. Jo is therefore asked to sit on juries for architectural competitions all over Europe.

https://jocoenen.com/cv/index.html

DO YOU SEE MANY NEW THINGS, AS A JURY MEMBER?

'No, but then again, that is not what we need, because what is new? Creating spaces is something we have been doing for a very long time, and when it comes to architecture or urban planning, innovation will only come from technological progress. Anyone who studies building history knows the classic example: the cast iron used to build the structures was later replaced by steel. But still with the same patterns, and using the same ornamentation. Just think of the Eiffel Tower. When you see what Brunelleschi [an architect and engineer from the Italian Renaissance] and many after him came up with in terms of technical innovation, you have to admit that progress is not necessarily the work of designers. This still holds true today, because steel was followed by reinforced concrete, which in turn made completely different shapes possible. And it goes even further now with the use of 'space frames', spatial structures that can take on all sorts of shapes.

I learned a lot about this in Germany, where great importance is attached to knowledge. At the age of thirty-four I was appointed professor there, and got to know colleagues with their bookcases full of history, among them technicians such as Frei Otto [German architect and structural engineer], Egon Eiermann, and Fritz Haller [Swiss architect and furniture designer]. I absorbed so much knowledge there that you could actually call it my second education.'

WE KNOW THAT YOU HIGHLY VALUE THE ART OF INTERWEAVING THE PAST AND THE PRESENT. WHAT IS YOUR VIEW ON CONTEMPORARY LIBRARY ARCHITECTURE IN THAT RESPECT? WE SEE THAT IN MANY NEW LIBRARIES THE COLLECTION HAS FADED INTO THE BACKGROUND. AS IF IT IS JUST A DECOR NOW.

'I place that in the category of freestyle wrestling. I have found my own footing, and do not want to give it up or trade it in for superficial discussions about experiences. I look at colleagues, but also at the world and think: I don't believe I have to go along with every ripple. I want to remain stable in my work. Maybe that will survive longer than the swaying and the wobbling.'

'It is not just about cataloguing, but making connections and thereby making things more interesting.'

WHAT IS THE STABILITY OF THE LIBRARY FOR YOU?
'First and foremost, I see the library as a treasure trove of knowledge. And then it's about teaching, about education. The library must therefore collect, and in doing so give the collection depth, bring out the historical context. It becomes really wonderful when the library sequences that, so that people understand it. An example: through my work for IBA Parkstad [the organization involved in the development of the Parkstad region in Limburg], I came into contact with former senator and architecture critic Nic Tummers. Tummers, who passed away in 2020, always used historical knowledge in his work; about architecture, but also about art, literature, and politics. He stored all of this in bookcases full of books and notes, which were arranged over two floors in his house in such a way that logical lines emerged, which he could use to teach. We have kept those lines, so that the next generation can draw from them and build on them. It is what we call fruitful knowledge, because it is presented in context. And that is what the library is all about: not just cataloguing, but making connections and thereby making things more interesting. Those lines can also be very personal, like personal archives that people keep. I relish that, and I noticed that young people also find it fascinating. So, when it comes to the question of what constitutes a library, it starts with that kind of 'archive', with gathering knowledge, and wanting to share it in order to be able to interpret current events. Even if young people who come to the library would get just a hint of that, I would already be pleased. Explanation, interpretation makes dead things come alive.'

'First and foremost, I see the library as a treasure trove of knowledge.'

WITH THE OBA YOU MANAGED TO MAKE THE LIBRARY WORLD PROUD AGAIN.
'For me, it began not only with the OBA, but also in Maastricht with the construction of the library in the Céramique Centre. There were three factors that made this library an example. I had the opportunity there to design bookcases myself, so that they could become classics. The second was that I was allowed to add an important public space, the main hall. And the third factor was that in that hall there were no restrictions to going further into the building, so no thresholds and no gates. It was a real battle to get that done, but it meant that everyone could feel welcome and just come in for a coffee. The alderman from Amsterdam visited Maastricht at the time and wanted a similar concept for her library. She saw it as letting go of the then prevailing typology, and in the OBA it worked out well!'

Beste vriendjes
Rikki
KAREL het Kuiken

SPEAKING OF TYPOLOGY, CAN WE DEVELOP A NEW TYPOLOGY OF PUBLIC LIBRARIES?
'So far, I've kind of avoided it, although I like the term. When you use the word typology, it is often seen as outdated, as an archaic concept. People associate it with Ledoux [French neoclassical architect who developed a strict, monumental style based on circles, rectangles, and triangles]. Or people picture old images, such as the design of the never-built National Library of Paris by Boullée. But if you start the conversation about typology these days, people want to turn the library into a marketplace.
If that is to be the new typology, I would rather not use that word anymore.'

IS A NEW TYPOLOGY POSSIBLE IN WHICH YOU DO NOT DISCARD ALL THE OLD? WE THINK IT IS VERY INTERESTING WHAT MUSEUMS DO NOWADAYS, CONSTANTLY CHANGING THE WAY THE COLLECTION IS PRESENTED, THROUGH DIFFERENT ARRANGEMENTS, DIFFERENT CONTEXTS, AND SO ON.
'Lately, we see more and more museums of private collectors. The tradition of collecting could also be an impulse in the library world. My very first commission as Chief Government Architect [Jo held this position from 2000-2004] was the transformation of the Rijksmuseum in Amsterdam. I immediately introduced a number of architects who were not on the usual lists. Including Cruz y Ortiz, the Spanish architectural firm that was ultimately chosen. Germans and Italians have extensive knowledge, but so do Spaniards.
I wanted to influence the culture, to break with a trend. Re-approaching the building from old traditions, down to the last detail. That worked out well and gives the building a kind of perpetuity. The building celebrates the collection. The historical context, the background, is not regarded as a coincidence. The library world should adopt the same approach.'

WHAT CHARACTERIZES A LIBRARY DESIGNED BY YOU?
'The hopes and the predictions I put into it. But it remains to be seen whether others recognize these. We architects think we can do everything: design buildings, squares, and streets that everyone thinks are a complete success from the start. That is what I call hubris, conceit. That is why I keep listening to what people say about it for years afterwards. Sometimes people surprise me, for example when it comes to the Céramique area. I have heard people say that I did them a great favour because they really feel at home there. The same with the OBA. I received a message from an American who had to spend three months in Amsterdam and wrote: I am so grateful to you, because I was able to spend every day in the OBA, and my time in Amsterdam was unforgettable as a result. That gives me confidence, because apparently my way of reasoning has caught on. To make a building is to set up reasoning, which is hypothetical. Through study, concentration, and deepening you try to reduce the degree of hypothesis about how the building will be used. That is the quintessence of the architectural profession. Do people understand it, do they recognize it, what association do they have with it? In the French Enlightenment, architects made minor changes to existing typologies that were also recognized by outsiders. That common language, or rather that grammar, did not survive, and that is why I am trying to redefine the grammar of architecture today. Because if you don't have something to hold on to, and

you come up against a lack of knowledge, you don't know where to start. So, I hope people will recognize what the building is for, and whether it is being used as intended. You can compare it to biochemistry. A biochemist mixes substance x and substance y, and then knows what reaction will follow. Stringing molecules together is comparable to what architects do. That you put together a spatial complex from a number of components, and determine how they interact and what effect that has. And then hope your prediction is right.'

> 'The location of a building is important, but what matters most is its content, what happens inside.'

THAT BIOCHEMISTRY IS YOUR SIGNATURE? THAT IS WHAT SETS YOU APART FROM OTHER ARCHITECTS?
'Yes, it has to grow. It is not clear beforehand what it should be exactly; you want to discover that during the design process. The location of a building is important, but what matters most is its content, what happens inside. That is a quest you can only make with a client who really wants to think about it; who knows how they want to organize it and has ideas about it. Learning from each other about the things you both know, and talking together until you find the solution. This building together is that (bio) chemistry that I love so much. That is how it was with the OBA in Amsterdam and the Centre Céramique in Maastricht. I am convinced that it does not work any other way.'

WITH YOU, THERE IS ALSO AN INCREDIBLY AESTHETIC COMPONENT. YOU ARE AN AESTHETE.
'That's right, I made drawings and sketches from an early age. After finishing secondary school, I didn't know what to do exactly. I wanted to be an artist, but my father said: get a diploma first, then we'll see. As an educator and philosopher, he had come across so many good artists who could not make a living that he wanted to spare me that. I thought OK, but then I can study architecture. Then I went to the Eindhoven University of Technology, and I recognized very little of the philosophy world, the books of my neighbour, who taught architecture and art history... Don't forget that I had been educated by the Franciscans in the spirit of culture, science, and very thorough knowledge. I have found my path, but I have developed an aversion to those who treat the mother of the arts with disrespect. I have always resolved to continue to think in my own way. During my travels, I visited many firms and buildings by architects such as James Stirling and Oscar Niemeyer – those taught me the most. Then you come home and you know: this is the way, no doubts, Jo.'

'What couldn't be built in Paris,

A conversation with

WI
MA

MVRDV

was built in Spijkenisse'

NY

AS

THE
ROOM

‘The energy inside ultimately determines the shape of the building.’

Winy Maas

On our way to meet Winy Maas

one of the founding partners of the world-famous architecture firm MVRDV[1], we already suspect that we will not only be talking about library design. This has everything to do with the visionary and inquisitive attitude of Winy, of MVRDV, and of The Why Factory, the think tank of TU Delft (NL) about future cities that Winy leads. We are clearly not only dealing with architects of buildings, but also of ideas. And that is one of the reasons why MVRDV is so renowned and operates all over the world.

1 https://www.mvrdv.nl

But to start with library architecture: we can read virtually everywhere that MVRDV has designed two libraries, the Boekenberg (Book Mountain) in Spijkenisse (NL) from 2012, and the Tianjin-Binhai library in China, which opened in 2017. Less well known is the design of the Brabant Library, one of the imaginary libraries created in 2000 as part of the Brabant Libraries 2040 project[1]. The 230-metre-high tower of this Brabant Library would house the ultimate provincial collection: almost five million books, placed in a spiral of 17 km of racks.

LOOKING AT THE BRABANT LIBRARY, THE BOOK MOUNTAIN, AND THE TIANJIN-BINHAI LIBRARY, WHAT DO YOU THINK IS THE COMMON THREAD IN THOSE DESIGNS?

'All three admire the collection; they monumentalize it. The collection is presented as thinly as possible; a single row of books, so that you can see all of them. Furthermore, they make the entire collection accessible. I have always said that I hate it when books are thrown away after a few years. That is why we have made a second layer in Spijkenisse. Above the 1.80-metre-high bookcases are the 'spare books', which are basically the written-off books. This enabled us to show more of the collection than was actually allowed. It does mean that visitors will need to use a ladder sometimes.

The second thing they share is the categorization. In the spiral-shaped Brabant Library the books are arranged from A to Z. You start at the bottom with the A and finish at the top with the Z. The Book Mountain is also a spiral, but there, the people from the library could decide for themselves how they wanted to arrange the collection. In Tianjin-Binhai we made a hundred rows, which is related to the hundred letters of the Chinese alphabet. It also simply begins with the first letter below and the last letter at the top.

The story of that library has taken on a special political dimension. When the images of what was called the most beautiful library in the world appeared on the internet, there was a huge hype. People saw that wonderful space where you can talk to others and pick up books. A place where knowledge is just there for the taking, in China no less. That made a big impression and was, I think, also seen as symbolic. But when people actually visited the building, there was a second media hype, and this one was really mega. Due to cutbacks of which we were unaware, visitors cannot access the upper bookshelves from rooms placed behind the atrium, because there is no fire protection there. As a result, only 15 of the 60 bookshelves contain real books; the rest are painted book spines. Of course, this caused a commotion, because people thought censorship had been applied.

I found what happened interesting, also for us in the Netherlands, because it touches on the idea that the library is a democratic facility where knowledge is accessible to everyone.
In China, of course, things are different.

Yet it was not negative. Of course, there were people who said: you can't do that, it's a fraud, you are literally painting us a picture. But the political effect was very interesting.
We could use those two hypes to improve things and make it clear what we wanted, namely a fully accessible library. This requires two things: adaptation of the technology and more books. But they don't really have that many books. Yes, hundreds of books by Mao and Chiang Kai-shek, but they are in a separate room. We gave them the series of books from The Why Factory as a present, but they were not accepted straight away because they had to go through the 'committee' first. So, you may want to display as many books as possible, but then you find out that, in the end, libraries are also political. And access to knowledge all the more so.'

1 Rob Bruijnzeels, Nicolien van Tiggelen, Bibliotheken 2040: de toekomst in uitvoering (Den Haag: Biblion, 2001)
2 Dutch politician, 1994-2015 member of the House of Representatives and the Senate on behalf of the Labour party.

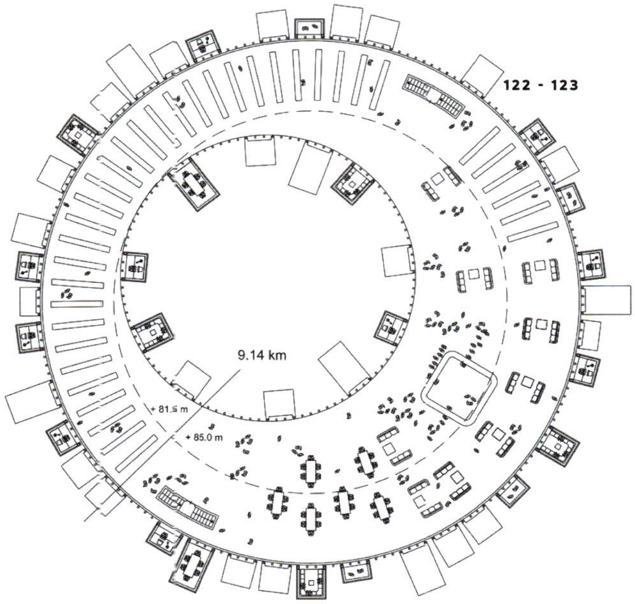

LOBBY

A CLASSIC EXAMPLE OFTEN CITED BY ARCHITECTS IS THE NEVER-BUILT NATIONAL LIBRARY OF PARIS BY BOULLÉE. IS THAT ALSO A SOURCE OF INSPIRATION FOR YOU?

'Yes, a little bit, but we are also thinking that this is the last moment that we can build a monumental library. The book will gradually disappear and soon it will only be about storage. You then get a kind of tomb, because everything will go through other mediums. But I suppose you know better than me how fast that is going.'

'You can design all kinds of wonderful search systems, but stumbling upon something by accident, is the most rewarding when you can walk past the books.'

THE BRABANT LIBRARY AND THE BOOK MOUNTAIN BOTH HAVE A SPIRAL COLLECTION ARRANGEMENT, THE ZIGGURAT. IN THE DESIGN OF THE MUNDANEUM, WHICH LE CORBUSIER ONCE MADE TOGETHER WITH LIBRARY VISIONARY PAUL OTLET, IT SYMBOLIZES THE UPWARD PATH TO KNOWLEDGE, THE IDEAL OF EDIFICATION.

'It's not meant that way. It is about two things: accessibility and search system. Monumentalizing the collection, making it accessible and visible, has led to a ziggurat. In Spijkenisse, this has even become an outward-facing ziggurat, as the Book Mountain is a glass library. I still like how Adri Duivesteijn[2] said when he visited the library in Spijkenisse: this is the most social-democratic building I have ever seen. That had everything to do with that accessibility, with being able to walk up slowly and see all the books along the way. The idea of the ziggurat was also used in the design that OMA, Rem Koolhaas' architectural firm, made for the Très Grande Bibliothèque in Paris, but which was ultimately not realized. You could say that what couldn't be built in Paris with the Très Grande Bibliothèque, was built in Spijkenisse.'

WE DO NOT FORESEE THE BOOK DISAPPEARING ANY TIME SOON. AT THE TIME OF THE LIBRARIES 2040 PROJECT, EVERYONE SAID THAT THE LIBRARY WOULD NOT LAST UNTIL THAT YEAR AND THAT THERE WOULD BE NO MORE BOOKS. BUT PREDICTIONS HAVE BEEN MADE BEFORE THAT HAVE NOT COME TRUE.

'Things are perhaps going a little slower than we had imagined. And it is still very nice to hold a book in your hands. And to be able to see them. You can design all kinds of wonderful search systems, but stumbling upon something by accident, which is of course also part of Google, is the most rewarding when you can walk past the books.'

'We need to think more fundamentally, and we can deepen that thinking by looking at examples from the past.'

WE ASK YOU SPECIFICALLY ABOUT YOUR SOURCES OF INSPIRATION BECAUSE IN THE WHY FACTORY BOOK 'COPY PASTE'[1] YOU WROTE THAT ARCHITECTS AND DESIGNERS ARE TOO OBSESSED WITH ORIGINALITY AND DO NOT PAY ATTENTION TO EXAMPLES FROM THE PAST.
'They do indeed disregard the knowledge of the past. Or, what I find even worse, they don't want to admit that they were inspired by others. They keep it to themselves because originality is so important to the client. My book calls for people to at least give references, as they do in other professions. It allows you to improve things. There have been very intelligent designs in the past, the library of Boullée, for example, or the Tower of Babel. We need to think more fundamentally, and we can deepen that thinking by looking at examples from the past. Thanks to technology, we can now make much better towers of Babel. Because we have search systems that can assist or sorting machines that move through the building. You can think of all kinds of things. Of course, it's not the only thing, those references. I dream of a three-dimensional matrix in which knowledge is stored in three or four axes. And then to be able to wander through it, that would be brilliant. And the massive library seems fantastic to me too. That it becomes almost like a distribution centre where you can get into every nook and cranny.'

AT THE SAME TIME, WITH THE WHY FACTORY YOU ARE EXPLORING THE HYPOTHESIS THAT THE FLEXIBILITY OF A BUILDING MEANS THAT THE FAÇADE WILL DISAPPEAR, AND THAT THE FUNCTIONALITY INSIDE WILL DETERMINE WHAT THE BUILDING WILL LOOK LIKE.
'Yes, the energy inside then ultimately determines the shape of the building.'

HOW WOULD YOU ENVISION THAT IN LIBRARIES?
'That's a good question. We have not looked into that yet. In the Barbapapa project of The Why Factory we are exploring how you can use malleable material to design buildings that adapt to the space you need. From the video Building Barbapapa[2], you can already see that this plastic material can become an information carrier. This material is electronically changeable, so it is easy to turn it into a super screen. And then any knowledge can essentially be accessed in the environment where you happen to be. The floor, the walls, everything becomes a screen. Information comes to you, where you want it. That's the ultimate Barbapapa story.'

1 Winy Maas, Felix Madrazo, Copy Paste: the Badass Architectural Copy Guide (Rotterdam: nai010, 2017)

2 https://www.youtube.com/watch?v=vJYDfKpKf8o (Accessed August 10 2021)

'The energy inside ultimately determines the shape of the building.'

THAT SEEMS EXCITING, A LIBRARY THAT REARRANGES ITS COLLECTION FOR YOU EVERY TIME.
'You can set preferences, like with Netflix, but you can also go further and fill in gaps in someone's knowledge or way of thinking. Then you bring an educational element into it, but I think that would be a good idea. I think it would be incredible for librarians to be able to programme that.

Barbapapa goes a little further. You can control the material with your voice or by touch, but also by emotion. This was tested at Design Week 2017. They wrapped a band around your head that measured your heart rate, brain wave and skin conductivity to see how you felt. These emotion data were fed back to a laser projection, which changed the colour of the smoke in the room. So that colour showed what emotional state you were in. There I discovered that the emotion is there faster than our awareness of it. I found this delay in awareness very interesting. I had never really thought about that. Imagine that librarians could tap into your emotion by showing you a particular collection. Wouldn't that be wonderful? I think it would be really cool to create such a space, where that collection comes to you through screens. The screens then form the building; that is one heck of an idea.'

天
海新区图书馆
HAI NEW AREA LIBRARY

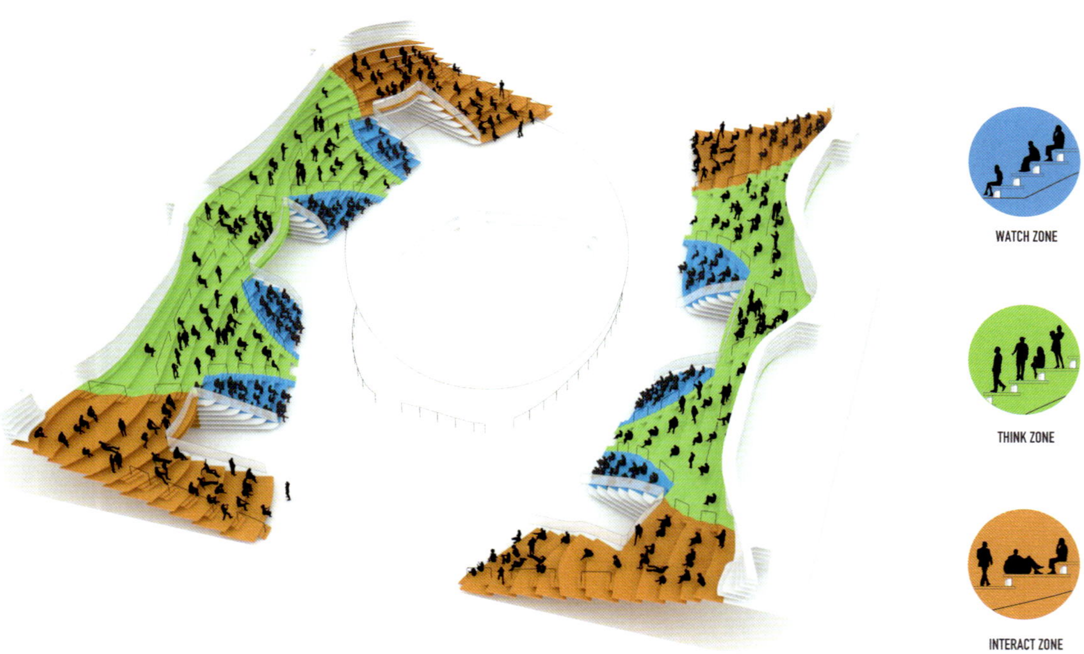

PERSPECTIVE 透视

foresee disappea-me soon.

IN YOUR DESIGN FOR THE DEPOT OF ROTTERDAM'S BOIJMANS VAN BEUNINGEN (THE WORLD'S FIRST FULLY ACCESSIBLE ART DEPOT, DATING FROM 2021), YOU HAVE CHOSEN TO SHOW WHAT IS NORMALLY HIDDEN IN STORAGE. WOULD IT BE POSSIBLE TO MAKE SOMETHING LIKE THIS FOR A LIBRARY?
'In a way, the Brabant Library was such a depot. And even more accessible than the Depot Boijmans Van Beuningen. The Depot is divided into fifty rooms, each with its own climate and technical facilities. This complicated things. And weight also plays a role. It is a super-heavy building, almost without windows, so there is a central void with six circulation routes where you can open different doors depending on the route you are allowed to take as a visitor. Some parts of the building are always open to the public, others only in certain seasons and still others can only be visited on request.'

SO AS A VISITOR CAN I CREATE MY OWN EXHIBITION THERE?
'Indeed. You can put together your own exhibition when you walk through it, because you are the one who makes the combinations. The curators will of course also make selections for the public space on top of the roof, the lower hall and the central void.'

WE THINK OF THE DEPOT AS A PROTOTYPE OF THE NEW LIBRARY.
'I think it's good that you're making this comparison, I hadn't thought of it that way myself. If you want to make everything public, including a library with delicate old books that require special climate control, then this is a kind of example.'

SOME ARCHITECTS ALWAYS INCLUDE A CLEVER JEST IN THEIR DESIGNS. SO DO YOU, RIGHT?
'Yes, that is usually present in our work. I like to tease a bit, like with the mirrored façade of the Depot. It reflects the surrounding buildings by other architects, so that it is also essentially Copy Paste. The fact that an enlarged barn was created in Spijkenisse is a reference to a town that wanted to become larger. And the Glazen Boerderij [Glass Farm, a multifunctional building on the central market square of Winy's birthplace Schijndel], which is almost twice the size of the average Schijndel farm, also touches that chord. That is in fact also a storage medium. The knowledge about forty farms and their inhabitants is encapsulated there in the glass panels of the façade. So, you see that with such an information carrier you can actually make a brilliant medium. The village did become better known because of it. This just goes to show that it is important to do something special. But the content, of course, is what it is all about. When is something that is cool, also something that is good?'

"When is something that is cool, also something that is good?"

mbineerde

A conversation with

CHR
VAN DU

S
IJN

'The library is still a monument to optimism'

OMA

**"I really believe that you are happiest when you find something you weren't looking for in the first place.
We try to capture that in a building by encouraging people to go a bit further and explore, in a natural and positive way.'**

Chris van Duijn

starbucks

The Office for Metropolitan Architecture

(OMA)[1], the prominent and influential architecture firm founded by Rem Koolhaas, can pride itself on an impressive series of library designs. That some of them were never realized does not make them any less famous. In 1992, OMA designed two libraries for Jussieu, the technical university in Paris. Although never built, Jussieu is considered to be ground-breaking because, as far as we know, it is the first time the library was presented as a landscape. Equally impressive is the 1989 design for France's national library, the Très Grande Bibliothèque in Paris, which was conceived of as a massive repository of digital and physical media. It too was not realized, but fortunately there was a turnaround in 1999 when OMA won the commission for the Seattle, Washington Public Library. This was followed by Bibliothèque Alexis de Tocqueville in Caen, France (2016) and the Qatar National Library in Doha (2017).

https://oma.eu

They continue to be involved in library construction, Chris van Duijn of OMA tells us. Chris joined OMA as an intern in 1995, stayed on throughout his studies and eventually became a partner in 2014. He has worked intensively on the libraries of Seattle and Caen, and as head of the Asia Office is now mainly involved in OMA projects there. In 2021 Chris was negotiating with China about a library in Chengdu. OMA had recently won the competition for a master plan for a university campus, on which the central and most striking building will be a library.

IN THE THIRTY YEARS THAT YOU HAVE BEEN INVOLVED WITH LIBRARY ARCHITECTURE, QUITE A FEW THINGS SEEM TO HAVE CHANGED IN YOUR OUTLOOK ON LIBRARIES. WE SEE A WORLD OF DIFFERENCE BETWEEN SEATTLE AND CAEN. OR DO YOU SEE THIS DIFFERENTLY?

'Yes and no. None of our projects look alike anyways. Sometimes the design is formal, other designs are more informal and very sculptural. We always try to get to the essence first. What is the project about? Once we are clear on that, a spatial concept will gradually emerge. We approach all our projects in this way. Seattle and Caen are indeed very different, but both are trying to make the library as visible and accessible as possible, with the aim of attracting many visitors. What makes a difference is that American public libraries have a broader social function than those in other countries. There, it is also a place where homeless people can stay warm and dry during the day, without being chased away. That context plays a part, as does the fact that you cannot compare downtown Seattle with the more rural Caen. So, the implementation is completely different, but the starting point remains the same, namely to establish the strongest possible relationship with the public and with the city.'

WHEN 'SEATTLE' WAS DESIGNED, THE PREVAILING OPINION WAS THAT BOOKS WOULD GRADUALLY DISAPPEAR AND THAT ROOM WOULD HAVE TO BE MADE FOR OTHER FORMS OF INFORMATION EXCHANGE. LATER ON, THOUGH, WE SEE BOOKS TAKING UP A VERY PROMINENT POSITION IN YOUR DESIGNS AGAIN.

'The most extreme example is perhaps the design of the Très Grande Bibliothèque in 1989, in which the building was stripped of all classical meanings and reduced to a cube, a huge repository of information. If you then look at the Qatar National Library in Doha, where the entire space is dominated by the presence of books, you will indeed see the opposite. A landscape of books has been created there in an orchestrated setting, which is also visible from the outside.

We never believed that books would disappear, by the way; only that things would become increasingly diverse as other media would emerge alongside them. The consideration always remains: what is the meaning of public space in a monument such as a library? Because you could say that the library is still a monument to optimism. And you have to make a physical translation of that.

Seattle, I think, is a combination. It has elements that can also be found in both Doha and Caen. The living room, for example, where the bookcases actually serve more as a setting. Only a few percent of the books are there, but they are important for giving you the feeling that you can browse through them. I really believe that you are happiest when you find something you weren't looking for in the first place. Serendipity, as they say. We try to capture that in a building by encouraging people to go a bit further and explore, in a natural and positive way. That is why circulation and the experience of the spaces are so important in our projects. In Seattle, this has been worked out in an urban way, while in Qatar it has become more like an oasis in the desert.'

'If you cannot clearly predict the future of the library, you will have to build in flexibility.'

IS THAT A GUIDING PRINCIPLE FOR YOU - THAT YOU DESIGN A LIBRARY ON THE BASIS OF SERENDIPITY? THE RESULT IS, OF COURSE, SOMETHING QUITE DIFFERENT FROM THE NEATLY ARRANGED CLASSICAL LIBRARY THAT IS GEARED TOWARDS FINDABILITY.
'Yes, but one does not necessarily exclude the other. In Seattle, for example, you find that both these approaches feature prominently in the design. Flexibility also played an important role in this. If you cannot clearly predict the future of the library, you will have to build in flexibility. But what is that? There is generic flexibility, where rooms such as the reading room, the conference room, et cetera, can change place, and there is specific flexibility where, for example, the books can be relocated. In Seattle, we applied the latter by designing a book spiral, a ribbon along which you can move the books if necessary. The rubber mats with numerical indication that lie on the floor then simply slide along. In addition, bookcases have been placed in the living room and the reading room, where you can find things you weren't necessarily looking for.'

IN YOUR BOOK ABOUT THE SEATTLE PUBLIC LIBRARY[1] IT SAYS THAT YOU AIM FOR A MORE SOPHISTICATED FORM OF FLEXIBILITY BY COMPARTMENTALIZING SPACES. SO, NO GENERIC FLOORS WHERE ANYTHING CAN BE DONE, BUT SPACES THAT ARE SPECIALLY EQUIPPED FOR THEIR FUNCTION. BUT IF THAT IS YOUR APPROACH, WHERE DOES IT LEAVE THE FLEXIBILITY?
'At the start of the competition, members of our team went to visit the ten most recent major libraries in the US at the time to see how they had handled the various themes. It turned out that all those libraries had a standard cross-section after all. The ground floor was a bit higher, but upstairs, all floors were the same height, on the pretext that you don't know if the collection will grow or if you will need more offices in the future. And then it turns out that the public areas, the reading areas, are limited to the entrance hall because it is a bit higher there, and that the rest actually looks like office space. We think public space is very important in a library and we wanted to celebrate it more, give it more meaning, so that it would also be very appealing to go into the library. In that respect, we were true optimists. It meant that we had to define flexibility differently. You do not need to be able to do anything anywhere. An office environment changes over time, but you can adapt to this quite easily by using flexible partitions. You can keep the storage and archive spaces low, because they do not require daylight. So, you don t have to give all spaces the same characteristics, but you can try to optimize them, as we did with the book spiral in Seattle. In those other libraries that we visited we saw that the sections were all neatly distributed over the floors. But if a particular collection is then expanded, there may only be room available on the ground floor, for example. At that point, the relationship between the space and the way the library is laid out is gone. Of course, our solution in turn excludes other possibilities, but this was our approach. You have the hard programme and the soft programme; that is what it is always about. The square metres, the number of books and such, versus the circulation space and the public space. You always lose square metres to necessary circulation, but if you make that part of the public space as well, you open up all kinds of opportunities to create something beautiful. While in other places you save space by making it as efficient and compact as possible. These are literally spreadsheet exercises that we do to ensure that the overall efficiency is the same, but that we can get many more wonderful square metres where it makes sense.

We also try to balance the equation in another way by showing where we pay a lot of attention to beautiful floor materials, for example, and where we just paint the concrete floor. This may seem to be of minor importance, but these are public libraries with public budgets that will be published. As an international firm, you tend to get a reputation for being overpriced and late. It is very difficult to get rid of such a stigma, so it is helpful if you can show in a public project like this one that this is not the case at all.'

1 Michael Kubo, Ramon Prat (ed), Seattle Public Library (Barcelona: Actar, 2005)

'We think public space is very important in a library and we wanted to celebrate it more, give it more meaning, so that it would also be very appealing to go into the library.'

WHAT WE FIND SPECIAL ABOUT SEATTLE IS THAT YOU HAVE TRULY INVOLVED THE STAFF IN THE DESIGN OF THE LIBRARY FROM THE VERY BEGINNING.
THE LIBRARY SEEMS TO HAVE BEEN DESIGNED IN HARMONY, EVEN THOUGH IT WAS A COMPLETELY NEW CONCEPT THAT DEVIATED FROM THE CLASSICAL PROCESS THAT A LIBRARY STOOD FOR.

'In Seattle, but also in Caen, I found the cooperation to be very good. Of course, we sometimes had conflicts with the people, and they also had conflicts among themselves, but we had regular meetings, visited libraries that they considered important, had discussions with department heads, et cetera. It helps enormously if you have a client who shares everything openly with you.

With public bodies this is, I think, more often the case than with commercial companies.

In Seattle, Deborah Jacobs was the driving force and visionary, also when it came to convincing people within her own organization. You really need someone like that in the organization. I have noticed that librarians can sometimes be quite conservative. In Seattle, I worked with Maarten van Severen on a design for the bookcases. Our idea was to hang the bookcases in the book spiral instead of placing them on the floor. We thought that was interesting because something that hangs looks much slenderer and more fragile than something that stands. It could also be used as a system to deal with the earthquakes, with the weight of the books serving as a counterweight. We thought it would be very nice, but the librarians wouldn't hear of it.

The special thing about Seattle was that they started out by looking for an architect to develop a vision with them. A design would then follow from that. This was fundamentally different from Caen where, in the French tradition, a competition was held and then the time was taken to choose a design, which you then proceed with. In Seattle, they started at the very beginning and wanted to work out the design brief together with us. In that sense, this collaboration was much stronger, because we started working together right from the start. What's great about this is that the result is also collective, so you don't have to defend your programme.'

SEATTLE HAS TURNED OUT TO BE AN EXCEPTIONAL LIBRARY, ESPECIALLY FOR ITS TIME. THIS IS PARTLY DUE TO THE FREEDOM YOU HAD TO REACH A SHARED VISION PRIOR TO THE DESIGN. BUT NOWADAYS AN ARCHITECT IS ALMOST ALWAYS CHOSEN ON THE BASIS OF A DESIGN. THERE IS ALREADY A DESIGN BRIEF FOR THE LIBRARY THEN, WHICH IN OUR OPINION IS SOMETIMES RATHER LIMITED IN TERMS OF IDEAS, BUT WHICH YOU HAVE TO WORK WITH AS AN ARCHITECT.

'These programmes are often written by the same consultancy firms and sometimes simply copied. We receive a lot of requests to enter competitions and they are often very much the same. You will be judged by it, so you cannot ignore it. As an architect, you then have the choice of deviating from the programme and putting forward a different, intelligent solution. You have to make these kinds of choices and accept that you will lose as often as you will win. We are not a firm that is good at designing façades. With us, it starts right at the very start of the process. That is what gives us the greatest satisfaction and also what sets us apart from others.
In that respect, Seattle has indeed been a touchstone for us. It made us realize that this is the approach to design that we believe in. It was on this basis that we developed AMO, the virtual non-architectural counterpart to OMA. It is a think tank that focuses on strategy, exhibitions, research, and publications in the fields of architecture, design, technology, media, and art.'

'Nothing exists

A conversation with

VINCENT PANHU

without a reason'

JYSEN

KAAN ARCHITECTS

‘A building should speak to people. It needs to be anchored in history, and not be fleeting.’

Vincent Panhuysen

NHUNG DAM
DUIZEND VADERS

Vincent Panhuysen of KAAN Architects

keeps on talking for a while after our recording device has been switched off. And it is perhaps this last piece of conversation that best expresses what is so characteristic of his designs. 'A building should speak to people', he says. 'It needs to be anchored in history, and not be fleeting. Because nothing exists without a reason.'

https://kaanarchitecten.com

This certainly applies to Utopia, the KAAN Architects-designed accommodation for the city library and the Academy of Performing Arts in Aalst, Flanders, which opened in 2018. The three-storey building, which covers a total construction area of 8068m², is characterized by a unique concept. The functions of the library and the academy have been fully integrated. For example, the books have been placed next to the dance and rehearsal rooms, and the same rooms also serve as study rooms during the day. So, it is a place where you can experience not only the richness of language, but also of music, theatre, and dance.
The name of the building refers to the ideal society described by Thomas More in 'Utopia', the book of which the first copy was printed in 1516 by Dirk Martens, a printer from Aalst. It is not the only link to the city's history, as our conversation with Vincent shows. During the design phase, he became an actual resident of Aalst for a while, so that he could understand the character and industrial past of the city. Because designing always starts with a quest, he says. Something that also appears to apply to his career, because Vincent did not enter the profession in the traditional way. After secondary school, he considered the conservatoire, but eventually decided to go to the furniture-making school in Amsterdam. He subsequently attended the art academy in Utrecht, and finally the academy for architecture in Rotterdam.

DOES YOUR WORK REFLECT YOUR FASCINATION WITH MUSIC, VISUAL ARTS AND MAKING THINGS?

'It is especially the exploration of large and small scales that has always fascinated me. I did all kinds of different internships during my studies. At the International Institute for the Urban Environment, I worked on the Fourth Policy Document on Spatial Planning. But I also worked for an architect where I really did the small things. I still love this zooming in and out. I thought I wanted to be an autonomous artist, but that means you have to ask yourself every day what you are going to do for whom. What is so nice about architecture: someone comes to you with a whole stack of papers and says: 'This is what I want'. And then you have a context and a brief, and you start working on that task. Then you try to find out what a building means for that place and try to understand for whom you are doing it. I discovered, of course, that in architecture you do also have to take an autonomous position. I still find this balancing act between autonomy and adaptation to the client's requirements exciting, as well as the balance between theory and the final product.
I have never regretted going into architecture, because you get to work in a different context every time. In a spatial sense, because everything you build, you build in a location. But also, because you work for different users every time. First it is an embassy, then it is a crematorium or a court house, and now I am working for the Marine Corps. You have to put yourself in the shoes of such an organization every time. Who are they, what is their identity, what do you have to make so that it works for them? Architects come, but also go, so you always have to ask yourself what the building will mean to its surroundings in the future, and how it will be used. That makes it a very dynamic profession.'

SO, WHAT IS IT THAT MAKES KAAN ARCHITECTS SPECIAL? WHAT IS YOUR TRADEMARK, YOUR SIGNATURE?

'That is the search for the very specific aspects of each commission. What is it about, what is the added value of what we are going to do in that particular location, and for the people who are going to use the building? This requires good analysis and a thorough understanding of cultural-historical values. But of course, you also have to look ahead. When the building is completed, that's when it starts, especially for a library.'

WHAT WAS IT LIKE FOR YOU TO DESIGN A LIBRARY, AS THIS WAS THE FIRST TIME YOU HAD BEEN ASKED TO DO SO?
'No, not the first time, because in 2012 we designed the Education Center of the Erasmus Medical Center in Rotterdam, with lecture rooms, work and study areas, and a medical library. Not just for students, because doctors and even patients also go there. Actually, anyone in Rotterdam can walk in, which gives it a nice mix between applied science and society. And the books, yes, they are used less and less there, but they still determine the signature of such a space in a very beautiful way. It feels like a library, and somehow that evokes something in people. I feel it too when I step into a library.'

WHAT DOES THAT EVOKE IN YOU?
'That it is something that belongs to all of us. And that it is a privilege to be able to use it. In the library you experience where you have come from and where you are going. It is the link between the past and the future. You experience respect for the past, for previous generations and their legacy. The same happens when you walk into a church. You feel that history around you and you think: yes, wait a minute, now I am in a place that really belongs to all of us, a public place that holds our collective memory.
If you ask me to draw up a hierarchy of important buildings, with my Catholic background I would rank the church first.
Second would be the library, and then perhaps in shared third place the theatre and the museum.'

'In the library you experience where you have come from and where you are going. It is the link between the past and the future.'

HOW DID YOU REALIZE THAT IDEA OF A PUBLIC PLACE WITH CULTURAL-HISTORICAL VALUE IN AALST?
'Every time I start a project, I try to understand all the layers of such a site. Aalst has a very rich history and the building stands on a location where many things have happened. You can ignore that context, but I choose to include it in the design of the building. Therefore, during the competition, we did as much research as possible into the cultural heritage of the place from our "attic" in Rotterdam. But I also went to a hotel in Aalst, and experienced what is special about that city. It feels so close, that industrial past, the generations of workers, the nuns who lived there, the world of Louis Paul Boon [Belgian author, born in Aalst, 1912-1979]. Many old buildings are still there, so you can still feel that atmosphere. But the grain-processing factories in the centre also give the city a raw and distinctive character. You see people from all walks of life walking around there. But the most beautiful thing about Aalst is the succession of little squares as you walk through the city. I imagine that as a huge network full of nodes. Each of these places has its own identity, and I saw it as an opportunity to add another place to it with the construction of the library. So, the library should not be just another building, but one of the nodes in the network, a place that connects the people of Aalst even more. Then, a new building would stand next to those other iconic buildings in the city, carrying the city's DNA while adding something to its identity.'

DOES THAT MEAN IT IS ALSO PRIMARILY AN URBAN PLANNING INTERVENTION?
'Yes, because I wanted it to be a public domain. I think that a library should literally stand at the heart of society, not at the edge of the city. But to make it a new node, we had to open up the area. The Pupillenschool [Pupils' School] — the monumental building with which the new building forms a unit — was a closed block that had no public relevance for the city. I spent a long time trying to figure out how to place the new building on that square. I could place it as a free-standing object in the area, but that would mean going up in height. This would create a number of little squares, but they would never get any sun and you do want them to be pleasant. We could have filled up the plot completely, and given the building as large an atrium as possible, but then there would be no remaining space around the building and thus no urban quality. That is why we opted for a box up against the Pupillenschool. As a result, the new building and the old building have become one and — in line with the character of Aalst — three

"To inspire, that's what it's all about, that is the keyword for a library."

little squares have now been created, so that is a very nice addition. In the end, we were allowed to design those squares ourselves, with a good lighting plan, benches, and everything. We have also created extra space around the building so that it is really in the middle of the city now. So actually, it is not three little squares, but one big square with three different entrances.
These access routes are important because they literally give you circulation in your building. The square extends, as it were, into the building, and the large windows mean that there is always this exchange between inside and outside.
The different spaces in the building also each have their own programme, so they are actually boxes within a box.
In the end, that is literally how it was worked out.'

THE COMBINATION OF LIBRARY AND ACADEMY FOR PERFORMING ARTS DID PRESENT AN EXTRA CHALLENGE.
'Yes, in that sense it was a different commission. It was not supposed to become a stately, classical library, because that would not bring all social groups together. The building should, so to speak, also inspire people who cannot read or make music, but who come to listen, dance or watch.
It is a bit ambiguous, because you do want to show that it is a library. You want people to be aware of the cultural-historical value, to respect it. And on the other hand, you want it to be accessible to everyone. One of the core values formulated by the clients of the new court building in Amsterdam [designed by KAAN Architecten and completed in 2020] was "gezagwekkend" in Dutch, something like 'generauthoritative', a word that does not actually exist. By this they meant that it had to have an air of authority and at the same time generate a feeling of trust. Such a contradiction is also present here. On the one hand, it commands respect for the collection, and on the other hand, it creates an accessible and welcome atmosphere.'

HOW WAS THAT ELABORATED IN THE BUILDING?
'I followed the zoning plan very carefully, because it already envisaged full integration of the various functions. The idea was to show the mix, the richness. People are dancing here, drumming there, and are reading over there. To inspire, that's what it's all about, that is the keyword for a library. The central void allows you to oversee everything. And around the void, the books are placed next to the dance and rehearsal rooms. That overview, all those books that are placed there, that's what makes it impressive.
We wanted to make this treasure visible from the city, during the day and at night. The large windows in the building's façade present a cross-section of the inspiring programme that takes place inside. It is actually a kind of diorama, in which we also refer to Thomas Moore's Utopia again. An image of that dream world, made out of mouth-blown white neon wires, hangs behind a large window so that it can be seen from outside. But it also works beautifully the other way round, because you look at the city from the inside through those large windows, as if they were postcards. Another eye-catcher, of course, is the "biggest bookcase in town", which is filled by the people of Aalst themselves. That eleven-metre-high and eight-metre-wide cabinet can be seen from the Grain Market.'

YOU HAD A SPECIAL BRICK MADE FOR THE FAÇADE.
'We make sustainable buildings, which is why we had a special brick baked with local clay in a local factory. That touches on the DNA of Aalst again. Almost all buildings there are made of brick, but making the brick thinner and twice as long gives it a con-temporary character. The windows are all set back very deep, so the building feels massive. This gives it real weight, and makes the library a serious public building. The depth, the thickness of the walls, the dark-brown window frames... Everything contributes and ultimately gives character to the building. You want it to have an identity, you want to realize:
'I am in the library of Aalst now.'

WHEN YOU WALK PAST THE CONSERVATOIRE IN A CITY, YOU CAN HEAR THE MUSIC BEING PLAYED. THAT GIVES A FANTASTIC SOUNDSCAPE. IS THAT ALSO THE CASE IN UTOPIA?
'Yes, that is wonderful. You also have this in Utrecht [NL] at the Mariaplaats, where you hear someone singing with a piano. But according to the current regulations, it must be made so that nothing can be heard outside, as this could be of nuisance to the local residents.
In the music rooms, you should be able to just play the drums and the cello, while someone is sitting outside reading a book. This all looks nice on a design drawing, of course, but such a mix of library and music school is very complex. One produces sound, the other demands peace and quiet.
We figured it out, but it did not come easy.
I do think that inside you will always hear something of the music, though, when someone opens a door, for example. That is fine by me. When you enter a library, it is never completely silent. In the Erasmus Education Center, there can be many people at the same time, doing different things, together or individually. They are not bothered by each other, because the acoustics are very pleasant. A good library should have that too. In that regard, I think the Uithof, the Utrecht University Library by architect Wiel Arets, is a wonderful example. So beautiful, the acoustics and the alternation of darkness and light.'

WE WERE JUST GOING TO ASK YOU ABOUT YOUR FAVOURITE LIBRARIES.
'Apart from the Uithof, which I already mentioned, I also like old libraries, such as the Real Gabinete Português de Leitura in Rio de Janeiro, with those black ebony bookcases. That is more that classic image you expect from a library. Bookcases from floor to ceiling, you are literally standing in a bookcase there. Books give the building the prestige of a library. I also think the British Library is very good. I visited it when I was working on Aalst. I mainly looked at how that library was being used. How people sit there working and studying together so nicely. That truly is a public space, and that social function is very important. To see and be seen is, of course, part of that. That is why we made that large atrium with the study spaces in Aalst.'

'You no longer go to a library to look up something. You go to a library to look for something you haven't found yet.'

OUR RESEARCH ALSO FOCUSES ON THE QUESTION OF WHETHER IT IS POSSIBLE TO CREATE A NEW TYPOLOGY OF PUBLIC LIBRARIES. HOW DO YOU SEE THIS?
'A public library should first and foremost bring people together. In that sense, Aalst is a very unique project because music, theatre, dance, and singing are mixed with the functions of the library. The building is thus almost a city in itself. People go there for a certain reason, and on the way there they pass the collection. This creates even more possibilities to make that connection. But the connection also lies in the location of the building in the city, and in the fact that people experience it as something that belongs to them all. You no longer go to a library to look up something. You go to a library to look for something you haven't found yet. Just like a museum, you go there to see something you don't know yet. To be inspired, I think that is something very essential. The same goes for contact between different generations; it is a place where every resident of Aalst can feel at home. But how does that manifest itself in a typology? That is actually a rather odd word. The library as a type always starts from a context. So, when you talk about typology, it has to have something to do with the DNA of that place.'

INLEVERSTATION

A conversation with

MIC

'We want to celebrate the

RIE

HIEL

ıblic nature of the library'

DIJK

NEUTELINGS RIEDIJK

'I think the library will continue to be a place where we obtain knowledge. The book and all its variants will continue to play a central role.'

Michiel Riedijk

Michiel Riedijk, together

with Willem Jan Neutelings, is the founder of Neutelings Riedijk[1], an architectural firm known for its design of expressive buildings. Striking examples are The Netherlands Institute for Sound and Vision in Hilversum, the MAS museum in Antwerp, Belgium, and the new town hall in Deventer, the Netherlands. Two public libraries in the Netherlands are also part of their oeuvre: Rozet in Arnhem and the Eemhuis in Amersfoort, buildings that differ significantly from each other except for their monumental wooden staircases. And it is precisely these differences that make us curious, because what do they mean for our search for a new typology for public libraries?

1 https://neutelings-riedijk.com

IS A NEW TYPOLOGY ACTUALLY POSSIBLE?

'You can have three discussions about this. First of all: what is a typology? The second question is: what is different from before, and how do you define that in relation to the building and its structure? And the third discussion is: what then is the library? To start with the latter: the tendency is to ask how the library sees itself in the future. Well, the library has been around for over 2000 years, so it will probably continue to exist for another 2000 years. What, then, is the library's essential characteristic, and what is different now all of a sudden? The first change is that the transfer of knowledge is no longer directly tied to a particular location. Digital technology allows you to access knowledge anywhere and at any time. Of course, you could just as easily argue that the library is still the place to find all that knowledge. But what you see is that knowledge has been partially detached from the artefact. In the past, knowledge was tied to books. Nowadays, this is certainly no longer always the case.

Furthermore, the way we define our public life is changing. This has to do with the current times, with neo-liberalism. The idea that everything has to be marketed, including the library. This implies a different relationship between what is public, what is collective, and what is private. More and more private elements are included in the library. Restaurants, coffee bars, bookshops, and other services of which you might say: does it actually belong in a library?'

WHAT DO YOU THINK OF THIS DEVELOPMENT?

'I believe that a library should by definition be public. It is one of the most public places we know in society. In our designs, we want to celebrate the public nature of the library; that is what I think of in terms of typology. That you genuinely feel that everyone is welcome there. Not only young people or the elderly, nor only highly educated or semi-literate people. Being there for everyone is an essential characteristic and one of the strengths of the library. That all sorts of things are now being added to it, such as a trendy coffee shop or a restaurant, is perhaps just a fad. Whether or not to privatize parts of the library, whether or not to include these kinds of peripheral phenomena... all this will change again at some point, but none of it will affect the essence of the library.

The public nature of the library is something I believe will always remain. And I think the library will also continue to be a place where we obtain knowledge. The book and all its variants will continue to play a central role. I also think that a lot of libraries, whether they are special libraries or large public libraries, will continue to anchor themselves to the real artefact. When you see how children or people with low literacy learn to read, literally with the book in their hands, then you know how important the presence of the book is. In my opinion, this is not only of crucial importance in terms of content, but also cultural-historically. You can read Bordewijk's [Dutch author, 1884 - 1965] work on the iPad, but if you have a first edition of his novel Bint in your hands, you will see that the design of the cover and the chosen font reflect the intent of that book at the time. It is simply amazing when you understand why it looked the way it did then, and what the difference is with how it looks now. That is why I think the book will always be found in the library. It is a fantastic medium for what the library has to offer.'

'The only thing that can change the nature of the library is the degree to which it is public, and the position of its collection.'

EEMHUIS

ONSTELLING ✕ WERKEN ✕ SCHRIJVERS ✕ BOEKEN ✕ WERKPLEKKEN ✕ MUZIEK
RINGEN ✕ THEATER ✕ CULTUUR ✕ GESCHIEDENIS ✕ ONTPLOOIING ✕ INSPIRATIE
VERHALEN ✕ ERFGOED ✕ KOFFIE ✕ KENNIS ✕ ZOEKEN ✕ TALENT ✕ CONCERTEN
de app van archiefeemland

→ Tijdschriften & Studie
2
→ Kranten & Tijdschriften
1

MANY LIBRARIES ARE ACTUALLY TURNING AWAY FROM BOOKS, UNDER THE GUISE OF CHANGE. IT REMINDS US OF THE QUOTE BY WILLEM DE KOONING[1]: 'I HAVE TO CHANGE TO STAY THE SAME', WHERE THEY ARE MAINLY CONCERNED WITH 'THE CHANGE' AND NOT WITH THE QUESTION OF WHAT SHOULD REMAIN 'THE SAME'.
'The library is under a lot of pressure from the government and cultural policies. All kinds of wishes and desires, obsessions and fears are projected onto the library. And in a way, quite a few qualities are attributed to the library. Facilitating lifelong learning, for example, and all kinds of things related to it. Politically probably very relevant, but it will never change the nature of the library. The only thing that can change the nature of the library is the degree to which it is public, and the position of its collection. In it, you can indeed see trends that reflect the changes over time. But it also reflects the struggle: how should an old and venerable institution such as the library present itself in today's society?'

NOWADAYS, THE PUBLIC NATURE OF THE LIBRARY IS OFTEN TRANSLATED INTO A 'COSY MEETING PLACE WITH NICE SEATS AND GOOD COFFEE'. BUT IN OUR VIEW, THE LIBRARY IS NOT JUST A PUBLIC SPACE, BUT A PUBLIC DOMAIN, A PLACE WHERE PEOPLE ACTUALLY MEET.
'You cannot make someone meet another person. When I go to the library to return my books or pick up my children, I am not looking to meet other people. Whether a building really becomes a public domain has to do with activation. You can very precisely identify places in the building that are suitable for storytelling and for internalizing these stories, and for creating new ones, which is also one of the essential characteristics of a library. A building has to facilitate these kinds of activities and, in terms of space, you can do that very well by creating places for five people, for fifteen people, for fifty people and so on.'

HOW DO YOU USE THE ARCHITECTURE TO SUPPORT THIS ACTIVATION?
'A space cannot enforce something. The space cannot make you listen, cannot influence whether the story is good or bad, whether you are moved by it or not. That is down to the speaker's eloquence. But the space can provide a context that makes you think: I am comfortable here and I can hear the speaker well. Architecture can create the conditions for this; it is an instrument that then needs to be played.'

1 Dutch-American abstract expressionist artist (1904-1997)

YOU ONCE SAID THAT THE HALLMARK OF NEUTELINGS RIEDIJK IS YOUR DESIGN INTELLIGENCE. THAT YOU ALWAYS REINTERPRET THE ORIGINAL BRIEF, BECAUSE THE FUNCTIONAL REQUIREMENTS ARE USUALLY TOO PRESCRIPTIVE.
'I think this is about the same thing. Suppose a space is requested that is ten by seven metres and three metres high. You can meet such a technical demand by creating that space, providing air conditioning, lights and so on. But you can also interpret it differently by looking at the activity you want to facilitate in that space. For example, if you want to set up a reading room, you have to think about daylight. You are still concerned with the technical requirements of the room, but you make the question more precise by saying: when you read to people here, light must fall on the page and the people who come to listen should not be looking into the light, because then they will not be able to see the speaker's face. Then you know that the reading room should only get light from above and not from the side. This way you put a twist on that technical question and end up with a better library.'

'A vision regarding public space is crucial. What can we do to activate our visitors, how can we define different gradients of publicness and privacy in our building?'

IS THAT ALWAYS IN DIALOGUE WITH THE CLIENT?

'Absolutely. It is crucial that the client has a vision regarding public space. That they enter into a dialogue with you about the question: what can we do to activate our visitors, how can we define different gradients of publicness and privacy in our building? Places where people want to sit by themselves to read or study, or a place where you can do something with a hundred people. These are all gradients that you can literally set out in a building by determining together with the client: this is a very public place, this is private, here I can meet someone and here I cannot.'

WHAT IS YOUR EXPERIENCE IN THAT REGARD WITH LIBRARIES AS COMMISSIONS?

'I think it went very well with the two libraries we made in the Netherlands. Of course, there is some tension in the sense that as an architect you sometimes want to turn left while the client wants to go straight ahead. But that tension is crucial. The client's perspective is the content of library work. These are very practical questions, such as the size of the collection and the space required, but also the almost metaphysical question of what a library actually is. The client has to share these questions with the architect in order to create a good building, otherwise it will never amount to more than a sum of square metres.'

HOW DO YOU LOOK BACK ON ROZET AND THE EEMHUIS?

'I think they have both turned out to be very good libraries. They were completely different projects. One is a detached building, the other is not. Rozet's lot is very narrow and that of the Eemhuis is very wide. Because of these different starting points, the buildings have also turned out quite differently. Whereas in the Eemhuis the public domain is really in the heart of the library, in Rozet it is on the periphery of the building. The large staircase and the spaces next to it are the public domain. These are two very distinct differences that each have their own intrinsic qualities.'

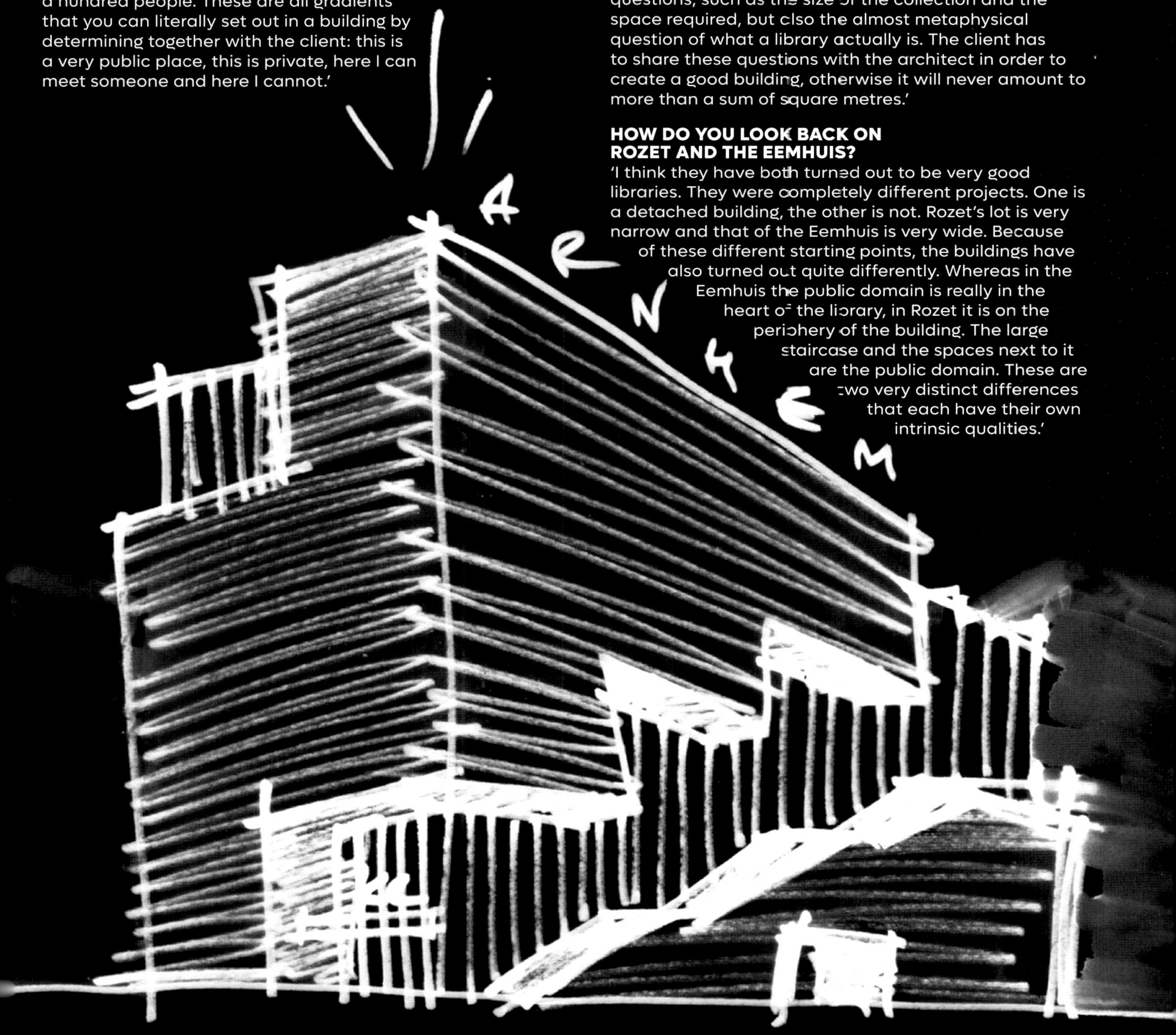

YOU ONCE SAID: 'PUBLIC BUILDINGS SUCH AS A LIBRARY SHOULD SPEAK, STAMMER, WHISPER, SING'. DOES THIS MEAN THAT YOU ARE ALSO CONCERNED WITH THE SENSORY EXPERIENCE OF A LIBRARY?

'One of the questions we asked ourselves when working on the Eemhuis was: what should a library sound like? You have this huge space there, with a perforated ceiling so it doesn't reverberate too much. And you have the lower rooms where part of the collection is displayed with a number of alcoves attached for even greater intimacy. So there are many different environments in the building, each with its own acoustics and sensory experience. I think it is very important to design from that idea. This also means that some rooms are made of concrete because reverberation is allowed there, while others are completely lined with wood to muffle the sound. In this way, you can calibrate the experience of a room very precisely and, at the same time, create big differences within a single building.'

SO YOU DON'T JUST DESIGN FROM A VISUAL AESTHETIC, BUT ALSO TAKE THOSE SENSORY ASPECTS INTO ACCOUNT?

'Yes, a building should have a layered quality. Just like it should tell a story. Without it being didactic, you have to be able to see: this is a library, you can have coffee here, you can read to your child there. You also need to have some kind of layering in the quality you experience. It would be very strange if everything had a uniform quality. You expect the toilet to look different from the auditorium.'

DOES THAT MEAN YOU CHECK ALL THE SENSES? HOW A BUILDING SHOULD SMELL, FOR EXAMPLE?

'Yes, absolutely, the scent of a parquet floor with beeswax, for example. And also how it feels to the touch, on account of the quality of the material. A public building should be welcoming and pleasant, so you don't want to feel sharp, unpleasant materials there. You don't have to draw attention to it explicitly, but you make it in such a way that people understand it, and have the right sensory experience with it.'

YOUR BUILDINGS ALWAYS HAVE THEIR OWN NARRATIVE, AND CAN ONLY BE IN THAT ONE PLACE.

'I think it is crucial that we achieve that. This is expressed in the shape of the building, its overall configuration, the use of materials, and the way it is organized. If you don't make something that is distinctive in those aspects, you won't get something that belongs in that place.'

SO YOU WOULD SAY THAT TYPOLOGY DEPENDS ON THE PLACE WHERE YOU ARE BUILDING?

'Yes, and so it does not necessarily depend on the nature of the commission. If you look at the Rozet plot, that strange wedge, you know that you could never have built the Eemhuis main hall there. So there is a direct relationship between the nature and size of the plot and the chosen typology.

In Rozet, we wanted to create a public street running through the building; that was one of our very first ideas. It was the only way to give that narrow building a public character. The idea for the rosette ornament did not come up till a year and a half later. Because it was such a complicated site in the centre of Arnhem, we had to make a prefabricated concrete façade that could be assembled quickly and easily. We thought that we could then also make a nice print in it, and looked for an artist who could help us with that. This shows that some ideas are there from the beginning, while others develop over time because you have found the right form.'

TO CONVEY THAT STORY, YOU ALMOST ALWAYS WORK WITH VISUAL ARTISTS. HOW DOES THAT WORK? DO THEY COME UP WITH THE IDEA? DO YOU?

'It really is an interaction. In the case of Rozet, we worked together to find a way to represent knowledge. This eventually led to the penrose figure, and the idea of putting that rosette motif on the building as a kind of stamp. The special thing about the penrose figure is that it has a geometry that continues endlessly, but is always slightly different.

An interesting analogy with knowledge.'

Bar

en, ontdekken, ontspannen en
www.rozet.nl
www.rozet.n
en in Roz

Bibliotheek
Wessel Knoops (1800)
Gerard Keller (1829)
Feest! Gratis dvd's en games

A NICE INSIDER'S JOKE, BECAUSE THREE OUT OF FOUR PEOPLE WON'T SEE THAT.

'That doesn't matter. A building has to tell a story, but you don't have to understand it. It is like a song you love the music of, even though you totally misunderstand the lyrics or the meaning. No problem. Sometimes when people hear that I am the architect of Rozet, they say: oh, that building with the stamps on the façade. It is great that someone has their own story to go with it, which is completely unrelated to the meaning of the penrose figure. A public building has to have an identity, to claim its own place, but that does not mean that everyone reads it in the same way. It would be absurd if the architect or the designer were to dictate the interpretation. A composer creates a piece of music and the reception of that piece of music always depends on the person who listens to it. You can think it is beautiful or awful, you can be moved to tears or just be annoyed. It is the same with architecture, but of course it is less powerful than music.'

IS THAT ALSO RELATED TO YOUR STATEMENT THAT ARCHITECTURE IS ABOUT THE BACKGROUND TO LIFE AND NEVER ABOUT LIFE ITSELF?

'Yes, because architecture cannot make people live in the right way. Architecture can only create conditions for life. There are buildings where everything is so neat and polished that you don't even dare to leave anything lying around. We have no desire to create that kind of prescriptive architecture. There have even been architects who wanted everyone in the building to have the same curtains. But you have to make a building where you can let life take its course.'

IMAGINATION

DON'T START BY REDESIGNING THE IMAGE; REDESIGN THE ACTION

Bruce Mau in Mau, B., & Ward, J. (2020). Mau MC24:
Bruce Mau's 24 principles for designing massive change in your life and work, p.444

TRANSITION:
VALUE:
TYPOLOGY:
PARTICIPATION:
INSPIRATION:
IMAGINATION:

I

PROGRAM OF IMAGI

"DON'T START BY REDESIGNIN REDESIGN THE ACTION"

We want to help guide libraries through the right considerations and choices during a complex building process, where many decisions have to be made in a short time. It is important to have a compass to keep you on track.

ME
IATIO

THE IMAGE:

When we design a library, we start with a Programme of Imagination, a practical framework in which we describe what changes we see in society, how these changes are reflected in a different way of working, and what this means for the design of a new building.

This is emphatically NOT about HOW a new library should look or the number of square metres it will occupy: those specifications will be discussed at a later stage in the programme of requirements.

FIVE STEPS IN TH
OF CREATING A N

How do we imagine a design proces optimal use of each other's creativ design a library, we start with a Pr which we describe what changes w in a different way of working, and w

The programme is divided int

1. *What is the essence of the public li*
2. *What is changing in our society?*
3. *How do societal changes affect pub*
4. *What does all this mean for the ar*
5. *How do you use your imagination*

PROCESS
W LIBRARY

n which architect and librarian can make qualities, and professionalism? When we amme of Imagination, a practical framework in ee in society, how these changes are reflected t this means for the design of a new building.

five parts:

ry?

library work?

tecture of your building?

nake it work?

WHAT IS THE **ESSENCE** OF THE PUBLIC LIBRARY?

A NEW LIBRARY IS AN INVESTMENT IN THE FUTURE. BUT WE CAN ONLY BUILD FOR THE FUTURE IF WE KNOW WHAT THE ESSENCE—THE MISSION—OF PUBLIC LIBRARY WORK IS. WHAT IS THE ENDURING VALUE OF YOUR LIBRARY, AND WHAT MAKES IT UNIQUE?

The mission guides the design process, and makes it clear to all those involved what the library stands for.

Clearly understanding your library's mission prevents everyone from succumbing to trendiness, or 'quick wins'.

A clear mission is the basis for a sound commission. Architect Nanne de Ru, founder of the Rotterdam-based architectural firm Powerhouse Company, states: 'Good architecture does not only require a good designer, but also a good client. There is no such thing as a good building without a good client.'

THE MISSION OF THE LIBRARY IN THREE CONCENTRIC CIRCLES.

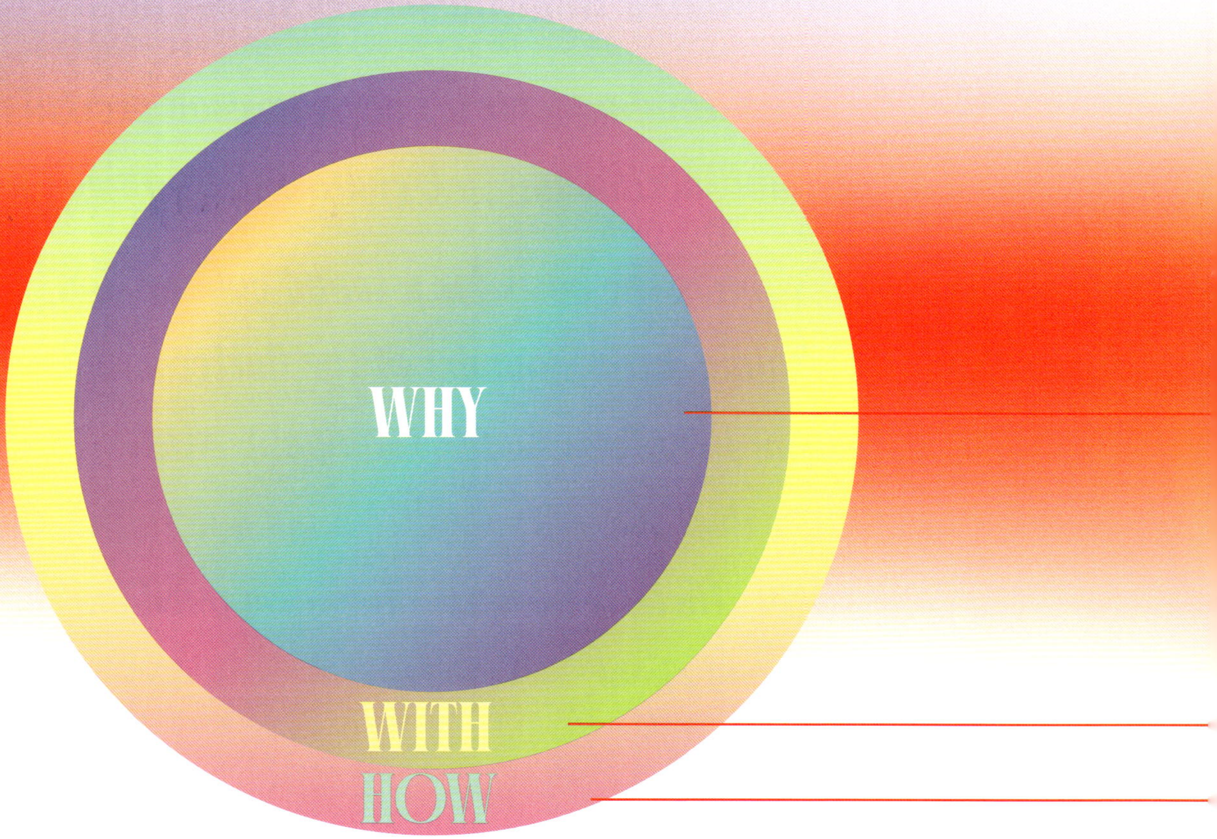

WHY

THE INNER CIRCLE DESCRIBES THE SOCIAL MISSION OF THE LIBRARY. THIS IS A FIXED AND STABLE VALUE THAT DOES NOT CHANGE SUBSTANTIALLY OVER TIME.

Contribute to the quality of the public domain through the provision of information, promoting:

- Freedom
- Equality
- Diversity

- Collection
- Building
- Staff
- Partners

WITH

THE MIDDLE CIRCLE LISTS THE RESOURCES (AND PARTNERS) NEEDED TO ACHIEVE THAT GOAL.

HOW

THE OUTER—MOST FLEXIBLE—CIRCLE DESCRIBES THE WORKING METHOD: HOW ARE THE RESOURCES DEPLOYED?

- Programming
- Participatory: with users
- Meaningful
- Safe
- et cetera.

PUBLIC LIBRARIES ARE OPERATING IN A SIGNIFICANTLY CHANGED CONTEXT. THE RISE OF INFORMATION TECHNOLOGY HAS HAD A HUGE IMPACT ON THE SUBSTANCE OF THE WORK. BUT THERE'S MORE TO IT: USER BEHAVIOUR IS CHANGING, SOCIETY IS BECOMING INCREASINGLY DIVERSE, AND NEW QUESTIONS AND NEEDS ARE ARISING THAT THE LIBRARY HAS TO RESPOND TO ADEQUATELY.

- WHAT IS THE 'BIG PICTURE', BEYOND THE ISSUES OF THE DAY, THE HYPES, OR THE TRENDS?
- WHICH CHANGES ARE RELEVANT, AND WHAT ARE THE NEW PARADIGMS THAT WILL GUIDE FUTURE LIBRARY WORK? THE AIM IS TO GAIN MORE INSIGHT INTO THE DESIRED TRANSITIONS.
- WE PRESENT THESE TRANSITIONS IN TWO COLUMNS, WITH THE LEFT COLUMN DESCRIBING THE EXISTING SITUATION, AND THE SECOND COLUMN INDICATING THE DESIRED NEW PARADIGMS.
- THIS APPROACH HELPS LIBRARIES TO IDENTIFY CHANGES SYSTEMATICALLY AND IN CONTEXT. IN DOING SO, YOU LAY THE FOUNDATION FOR YOUR OWN PLAN FOR CHANGE.

TOWARDS A NEW ROLE IN SOCIETY.

from	to
Information abundance	Interpretation and meaning
Consumption	Creation
Genius	Scenius
Self-reliance	Community spirit
Neutral	Engaged

WHAT IS CHANGING IN OUR SOCIETY?

HOW DO SOCIETAL CHANGES AFFECT PUBLIC LIBRARY WORK?

Changes in society and new technologies require a different way of working, with a central role for the library user, a different use of the collection, and new forms of collaboration. The library will organize its resources and knowledge to help the user participate as a full and engaged citizen in our society.

- **What new roles will collection and programming play?**
- **How can partners and future co-residents strengthen these roles? (and vice versa...)**

TOWARDS A DIFFERENT WAY OF WORKING

from	to
Content	Context
Product	Process
Distribute	Programme
Collection as a final product	Collection as a resource
Stand-alone	Cooperation

A different library process

parti

**For librarians, the new way of working is a process in which the creation and sharing of knowledge is central.
It is a cyclical process that involves creating meaning around the collection, adding new context, and challenging visitors to discover and share connections and insights.**

Library users have a completely different role in the new work process. They are no longer seen as customers or consumers, but as active participants in a process in which everyone can learn from everyone.

In an intelligent collectivity! it's not the library or the librarian that makes a collection valuable; it's what the users are contributing!

When designing a library, we regard the future users primarily as experts, curators, designers or... librarians.

STEP 3

WHAT DOES ALL THIS MEAN FOR THE ARCHITECTURE OF YOUR BUILDING ?

A NEW WAY OF WORKING PLACES DIFFERENT DEMANDS ON THE FUTURE BUILDING. IT REQUIRES A BUILDING AND A LAYOUT THAT ALLOW FOR DIFFERENT PROGRAMMING. THE LIBRARY WANTS TO CREATE RICHNESS AND SURPRISE, AND TELL STORIES WITH ITS COLLECTION.

- **WHAT DOES A DIFFERENT WAY OF WORKING MEAN FOR THE SPATIAL ARRANGEMENT AND PLACEMENT OF THE COLLECTION?**
- **WHAT MAKERSPACES WILL THERE BE?**
- **WHAT DO OTHER PARTNERS ADD TO THE BUILDING IN TERMS OF FUNCTIONALITY, AND WHICH SPACES CAN BE SHARED?**

TOWARDS A DIFFERENT LIBRARY BUILDING

from	to
Clear and controllable	Adaptive and β
Partners separated	Partners integrated
Media in one place	Media omnipresent
Airspace	Heterotopia
(Passive) Common space	Makerspaces

for the building

THERE ARE DIFFERENT FORMS OF 'COHABITATION'

Will other organizations or institutions be sharing the building? Living together can be done in many ways, ranging from 'living together apart' to the most comprehensive form: complete spatial and programmatic integration. The latter has the most advantages structurally (and financially), but requires a far-reaching commitment from all partners to also share work processes.

STEP 4

Shared front-door

(HOUSED IN THE SAME BUILDING, BUT NO OTHER SHARED USE OF SPACES)

Shared 'back office' facilities

(MANAGEMENT, CANTEEN, WI-FI, OFFICE SPACE, MEETING ROOMS)

Shared public areas

(ENTRANCE, THEATRE, RESTAURANT)

PARTNERS ARE SPATIALLY AND PROGRAMMATICALLY INTEGRATED

AIRSPACE OR

All over the world, trendy shops, coffee bars and hotel lounges are starting to look more and more alike. The American journalist Kyle Chayka calls this uniform combination of stylistic elements 'Airspace', by which he means a sterile aesthetic that makes all public buildings—whether they are libraries, airports, hotels, cafés or cinemas—uniform, impersonal, ostentatiously comfortable, and interchangeable. But how do you recognize a library in that world of uniformity?

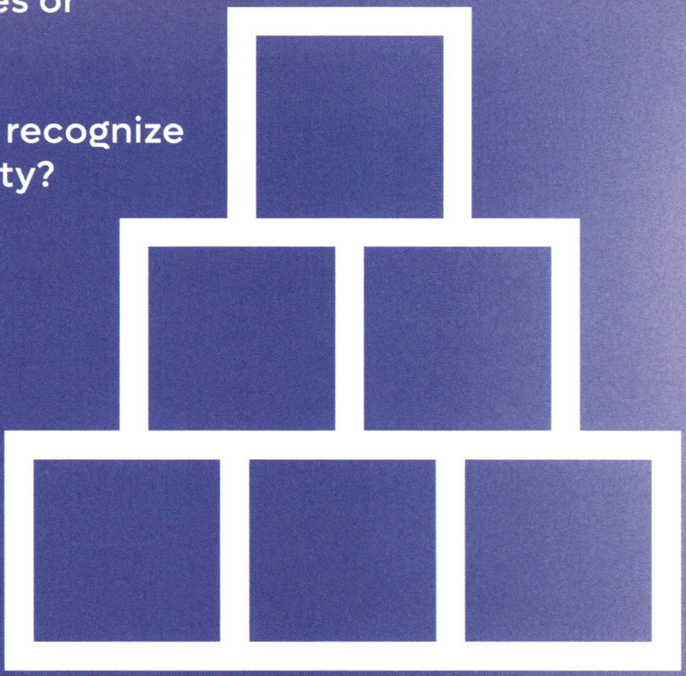

HETEROTOPIA?

A characterization that better captures the meaning and complexity of what goes on in our dream library is heterotopia, which literally means 'other place'. The philosopher Michel Foucault coined this term to describe spaces reserved for something special, out of the ordinary. It is an inbetween space, a place where you can grow, and where your perspective can change through interaction with other people and other cultural expressions.

MAKE IT WORK!

Expectations and assumptions play a major role in designing a new library. But will everything work as planned? And how are users going to react to that? The best way to find out is to explore other ways of working in a laboratory for new library work. There you can test all kinds of concepts and ideas, and see how users react to them.

- *It becomes clear what requirements the various makerspaces have to meet.*
- *You can build support for new ideas and concepts, and gain insight into whether the organization and its employees are sufficiently prepared for change.*
- *You have an excellent opportunity to discover how the collaboration with the partners can be organized.*

How do you use your imagination to make it work?

INNOVATION REQUIRES DIFFERENT STRATEGIES

Improve
DO THE SAME THING BETTER

Change
DO THE SAME THING DIFFERENTLY

Innovate
DO DIFFERENT THINGS

Each form of innovation has its own specific approach. Depending on the challenge, capacity and resources are used differently:

If the existing situation needs to be improved (e.g., longer opening hours), it is often a matter of reaching an agreement and implementing it.

• For more complex changes (e.g., a new catalogue system or digital services), c project plan is made.

• But when it comes to completely new things, a strategy of imagination is called for: experiments are used to find out whether these new ideas work, and how the users react to them.

THINGS TO CONSIDER WHEN EXPERIMENTING

ORGANIZATION AND STAFF

• Innovating means stepping off the beaten track, and not everyone is comfortable with that; it is by definition a disruptive process.
One should avoid going too far outside the comfort zone of the employees, but instead expand that comfort zone with imagination.

• Not only should the 'creative vanguard' of employees be involved in the project design, but also those who are less enthusiastic. Change works best when it becomes an attractive and creative challenge that appeals to different talents in an organization. Organizing this critical exchange of views also prevents the not-invented-here syndrome.

• Experimentation is teamwork that benefits from trust rather than hierarchy. Mistakes will be made; do not penalize staff for making them, but find ways to learn from mistakes together.

USERS

• Library users should be taken seriously because they can improve a design with valuable 'user experience'.
• However, it should be borne in mind that users cannot immediately imagine what new concepts and plans might look like. Remember the famous quote by car maker Henry Ford: 'If I had asked people what they wanted, they would have said faster horses.'
• It is better to develop and test new concepts in an experimental setting with users.
• Experimentation is also a good method to inform users about new building plans, and to involve them in these plans.

SETTING UP THE PROCESS

• New ideas and concepts should be approached methodically, distinguishing different steps, which should not be mixed up.

• It is important to set clear goals, and work with concrete 'hands-on' projects.

• A project becomes so much better when designers and other experts are involved in its design and evaluation.

• The principle of 'learning by doing' is essential; this happens in a laboratory for new library work, where people can experiment to their heart's content. In anticipation of their new buildings, the libraries of Århus (Transformation Lab) and Tilburg (Kennismakerij) started laboratories in which they could experiment for a number of years with new innovative forms of library work. Their tested ideas were later implemented in Dokk1 and the LocHal, respectively.

The four most important steps in experimentation

USABLE?

IN PILOTS, YOU CAN INVESTIGATE WHETHER AND HOW USERS REACT TO AND USE THE PROTOTYPE, AND WHAT THAT MEANS FOR APPLICATION IN A NEW BUILDING.

POSSIBLE?

THE FIRST STEP IS TO USE PROTOTYPES TO CHECK WHETHER THE IDEA IS TECHNICALLY DOABLE, AND WHAT IS NEEDED IN TERMS OF SPACE, EQUIPMENT, AND FINANCES DURING THE EXPERIMENT.

STEP 5

YOU DON'T JUST EXPERIMENT AT RANDOM. A METHODICAL APPROACH IS USED TO EXAMINE THE MOST IMPORTANT QUESTIONS.

SCALABLE?

CAN THE NEW IDEA DEFINITELY BE IMPLEMENTED BEYOND THE TEST LAB, AND WHAT ARE THE PRECONDITIONS (ORGANIZATION, FINANCES, REQUIRED SPACE AND EQUIPMENT)?

FEASIBLE?

IS THERE SUFFICIENT SUPPORT FROM THE ORGANIZATION, PARTNERS, AND EMPLOYEES? ARE THEY ABLE AND WILLING TO WORK WITH THE NEW CONCEPT?

MAKE IT WORK!

Possible themes

Collection

- How can you and the users create 'new storylines' with the collection?
- How can you design new and appealing ways to present the collection?
- How can users see what themes the library is working on, and what the results are?

POTENTIAL PARTICIPANTS:
STORYTELLERS
CURATORS
DESIGNERS

City

- In a citylab, explore the future of the city with all possible data generated.
- City of stories: what stories does the city hold, and how do you make them visible in the collection?
- What are the seven sins, virtues, and so on of the city, and how are they reflected in the collection?

POTENTIAL PARTICIPANTS:
DATA ANALYSTS
HISTORIANS
ANTHROPOLOGISTS

to experiment with

Building

- WHAT NARRATIVE DO YOU TELL IN THE BUILDING, AND HOW DO YOU DO THAT?
- DESIGN ACCOMMODATION SCENARIOS FROM DIFFERENT USER PERSPECTIVES: WANDERER, PARTICIPANT, RESEARCHER, ET CETERA.
- EXPLORE THE BUILDING WITH ALL YOUR SENSES; E.G., WHAT WILL THE BUILDING SMELL LIKE, FEEL LIKE, WHAT WOULD I LIKE TO EAT THERE?

POTENTIAL PARTICIPANTS:
STORYTELLERS
CURATORS
FRAGRANCE DESIGNERS,
CHEFS, ET CETERA.

Children

- HOW DO YOU MAKE THE BEST USE OF CHILDREN'S TALENTS TO OPEN UP THE COLLECTION AND SHARE KNOWLEDGE?
- WHAT ARE THE REQUIREMENTS FOR MAKERSPACES FOR CHILDREN?
- DESIGN A TRAINING CURRICULUM FOR CHILDREN WHO WOULD LIKE TO BE LIBRARIANS.

POTENTIAL PARTICIPANTS:
CHILDREN
EDUCATORS
DESIGNERS

EVER TRIED.
EVER FAILED.
NO MATTER.
TRY AGAIN.
FAIL AGAIN.
FAIL BETTER.

[SAMUEL BECKETT]

IS IT OKAY TO MAKE MISTAKES?

Managers often say: 'it is okay to make mistakes'; because 'you can learn from mistakes'. That is easier said than done, because nobody likes to make mistakes, as they are about 'faults', and can be blamed on you. Perhaps it is therefore better not to speak of 'mistakes' or 'errors' in experiments, but of 'failures' from which we can learn.

Amy C. Edmonson (Harvard Business School) has been researching psychological and social safety in companies for years. She sees experimentation as an excellent means of exploring new things through 'intelligent and deliberate failure': 'Intelligent failures occur when experimentation is necessary: when answers are not knowable in advance because this exact situation hasn't been encountered before and perhaps never will be again. "Trial and error" is a common term for the kind of experimentation needed in these settings, but it is a misnomer, because "error" implies that there was a "right" outcome in the first place. At the frontier, the right kind of experimentation produces good failures quickly.

In contrast, managers in charge of piloting a new product or service—a classic example of experimentation in business—typically do whatever they can to make sure that the pilot is perfect right out of the starting gate. Ironically, this hunger to succeed can later inhibit the success of the official launch. Too often, managers in charge of pilots design optimal conditions rather than representative ones. Thus, the pilot doesn't produce knowledge about what won't work.'

DESIGN REQUIRES IMAGINATION!

DESIGNING NEW CONCEPTS IS A COMPLEX TASK, IN WHICH IT IS NOT CLEAR IN ADVANCE WHETHER ANYTHING WILL WORK AS INTENDED: EVERYTHING IS NEW AND UNKNOWN. AS A RESULT, EXPERIMENTS ARE OFTEN SURROUNDED BY UNCERTAINTY, DOUBT, AND FEAR. IT DOES NOT HELP TO JUST USE 'COMMON SENSE' WITH 'MORE OF THE SAME' AS THE ULTIMATE RESULT. WE NEED IMAGINATION TO ESCAPE THIS TRAP, FOR IMAGINATION EXPLORES THE DESIRABLE AND PERHAPS THE IMPOSSIBLE: THE DREAM.
SO, START WITH THE IMAGINATION, THE DREAM TO UNLOCK THE FUTURE, AND THEN TRANSLATE THAT BACK INTO THE REALITY OF EVERY DAY.

Brennan's Hierarchy of Imagination.

WORK WITH DESIGNERS ON IMAGINATION!

A challenge for designers is that the library is haunted by memories: we all know from personal experience what it looks like and how it feels. I can see it before me; I can smell it and still hear its sounds. It is that kind of experience that makes the library feel so close to my heart. Whatever the library is, it has a place in our mind, and it's hard to beat the images of my own memory. Often that memory of everything 'library' is so vivid that it prevents us from coming up with new ideas.
While we aim for a design that fits tomorrow we are restrained by our mind that is filled with the images of yesterday and today. Designers may take these memories as an inspiration and build on their strength, but ultimately their designs need to inspire imagination and point a direction to the future.

In memory of Bert Mulder (1952 - 2020)

EPILOGUE

'Nothing is lost, nothing is created,
everything is transformed'

EPILOGUE:

7

Epilogue

The world changes, the library changes, and so we need a different architecture. This could be a very brief summary of this book.
It took us about eighteen months to write it all down, and we experienced this as a creative and intensive period, during which we examined, evaluated, honed, and reformulated our own ideas.
The common thread was the value of the library as an exceptional public space where meaningful collections and programming are used for genuine exchange between different social groups. This makes the library essential to the social and cultural vitality of a community.
From the many conversations we had with colleagues, experts, and architects, we learned that this unique position calls for a design process that focuses on the specific rather than the generic. It no longer suffices to describe the library as a Third Place, Agora, or Living Room of the City. There are many institutions that present themselves as such, so such classifications do not make it sufficiently clear what the real added value of the public library is.
The design process of a library is complex. It requires focus, sharpness, and in-depth knowledge of what distinguishes a library from all those other providers in the information, knowledge, and leisure market.
At the same time, we felt a growing urgency to reinvent the library without losing sight of its core values. A 'next library' in which inspiration, creation, and participation are central. Architects can create the necessary space for this, both literally and figuratively. Library innovation can become a truly exciting team effort when architects, librarians, and designers work together and bring out the best in each other. We discovered that architects can be excellent storytellers and advocates for public library work. But above all, they are—in the words of the Dutch Chief Government Architect Floris van Alkemade—'specialists in change'.

Very often, we asked ourselves what makes for a good library, what are its essential characteristics. In the end, we narrowed things down to three aspects: a good collection, a good building, and good staff. What future library work will require from employees is not addressed in this book. This was a deliberate choice, because this book is, after all, about architecture. Perhaps there will be another book that looks more closely at the organization and the competences needed to make the new way of working a success.
We were also unable to measure the impact of the new forms of library work we are advocating. The experiences with it are still too fresh and too diverse for in-depth analysis. Another factor is that there are hardly any distinguishing measuring criteria and key data available to evaluate 'new library work'. We believe that these will need to be developed and we sincerely hope that our book will provide inspiration and new research material for this.
And finally, we began our journey of discovery into the library of the future under the motto: 'I have to change to stay the same.' Under the influence of technological and social changes, the library will have to keep innovating. And that invariably calls for a new architecture to support that process.
Nobody knows what the library will look like in a hundred years. But what it ultimately stands for will always remain the same: the deep human need for imagination, the desire to tell each other stories, the constant search for meaning and direction in our lives, and the connection with all those others around us, who also want to participate in society out of curiosity and engagement. In our journey into the future, we will have to navigate between tradition and change. But whatever happens, it is a transition that preserves the same value: 'Nothing is lost, nothing is created, everything is transformed'.[1]

1 Antoine Lavoisier, French chemist (1743 - 1793) who established the law of conservation of mass.

Last but not least, we would like to thank all friends, colleagues and others without whom it would not have been possible to make this book:

- Our fellow ministers in the Ministry of Imagination: Jan David Hanrath, Florian de Visser, and Marien Brand for all their ideas and continuous commitment.
- The group of 'critical co-readers', who kept us on our toes while writing:
    - Eimer Wieldraaijer, former editor-in-chief of Bibliotheekblad (the Dutch Public Library Magazine), who gave us the idea of interviewing architects.
    - Frans Meijer, who made the initial contact with the publisher to make the publication of this book possible.
    - Jeanine Deckers, library director and architectural historian, and Dolf Broekhuizen, architectural historian, in particular for their expert advice when we were describing library typologies.
- Mari Nelissen and Rammy Speyer, for their help in creating the Programme of Imagination.
- Laurie Putnam, for the many years of inspiration, her expert advice and tremendous editorial help.
- All the architects we spoke with.
- Marjo van Schaijk, for her insightful input when we were describing the value of the library in the urban environment.

Thanks

Photo and Illustration

24	LocHal Tilburg (NL)	Stijn Bollaert
26-27	LocHal Tilburg Stairs (NL)	Rob Bruijnzeels
28-29	LocHal Tilburg (NL)	Stijn Bollaert
31	LocHal Tilburg (NL)	Stijn Bollaert
32-33	LocHal Tilburg (NL)	Stijn Bollaert
34	Groninger Forum (NL)	Marcel van der Burg
35	Groninger Forum (NL)	Courtesy of NL Architects
36-37	Groninger Forum (NL)	Marcel van der Burg
38-39	Groninger Forum (NL)	Marcel van der Burg
40-41	Groninger Forum (NL)	Roos Aldershoff
52	LocHal Tilburg (NL) Information desk	Rob Bruijnzeels
63	Le 104 Paris (FR)	Alamy
64	Chocolate Factory Gouda (NL)	Ministerie van Verbeelding
65	Chocolate Factory Gouda (NL)	Ministerie van Verbeelding
66-67	Chocolate Factory Gouda (NL)	Florian de Visser
68-69	Emmeloord Central Station (NL)	Florian de Visser
76	Ralf Coussée and Klaas Goris	Courtesy of Coussée Goris Huyghe architecten
78	De Krook Ghent (BE)	Courtesy of RCR Arquitectes
80-81	De Krook Ghent (BE)	Tim Van de Velde
82-83	De Krook Ghent (BE)	Tim Van de Velde
85	De Krook Ghent (BE)	Courtesy of RCR Arquitectes
86	De Krook Ghent (BE)	Tim Van de Velde
90	Francine Houben	Renée Klein for Bibliotheekblad
92	Birmingham UK Public Library (GB)	Harry Cock, Courtesy of Mecanoo
94-95	Birmingham UK Public Library (GB)	Harry Cock, Courtesy of Mecanoo
96-97	Stavros Niarchos Foundation Library New York	Courtesy of Mecanoo
99	Stavros Niarchos Foundation Library New York	Max Touhey, Courtesy of Mecanoo
100-101	Birmingham UK Public Library (GB)	Harry Cock, Courtesy of Mecanoo
104	Jo Coenen	Renée Klein for Bibliotheekblad
106	OBA Amsterdam (NL)	Courtesy of Jo Coenen
108	Centre Ceramique Maastricht (NL)	Christian Richters, Courtesy of Jo Coenen
109	Centre Ceramique Maastricht (NL)	Courtesy of Jo Coenen
110-111	OBA Amsterdam (NL)	Luuk Kramer
112	OBA Amsterdam (NL)	Alamy

credits

113	OBA Amsterdam (NL) Sketch of youth department	Courtesy of Jo Coenen
114-115	OBA Amsterdam (NL)	Luuk Kramer
118	Winy Maas	Renée Klein for Bibliotheekblad
120	Book Mountain Spijkenisse (NL)	Jeroen Musch, Courtesy of MVRDV
122-123	Brabant Library	Courtesy of MVRDV
123	Brabant Library	Courtesy of MVRDV
124-125	Brabant Library	Courtesy of MVRDV
126	Book Mountain Spijkenisse (NL)	Dario Scagliola & Stijn Brakkee
128-129	Tianjin Binhai Library (CN)	Ossip van Duivenbode, Courtesy of MVRDV
130	Tianjin Binhai Library (CN)	Ossip van Duivenbode, Courtesy of MVRDV
130	Tianjin Binhai Library (CN) Diagram activities	Courtesy of MVRDV
132-133	Museumdepot Rotterdam (NL)	Ossip van Duivenbode, Courtesy of MVRDV
134-135	Museumdepot Rotterdam (NL)	Ossip van Duivenbode, Courtesy of MVRDV
138	Chris van Duijn	Fred Ernst, Courtesy of OMA
140	Seattle Central Library (US)	Philippe Ruault, Courtesy of OMA
142-143	Seattle Central Library (US)	Philippe Ruault, Courtesy of OMA
144-145	Qatar National Library (QA)	Delfino Sisto Legnani and Marco Cappelletti, Courtesy of OMA
147	Bibliothèque Alexis de Tocqueville Caen (FR)	Delfino Sisto Legnani and Marco Cappelletti, Courtesy of OMA
148-149	Jussieu – Two Libraries	Hans Werlemann, Courtesy of OMA
152	Vincent Panhuysen	Renée Klein for Bibliotheekblad
154	Utopia Aalst (BE)	Dirk Verwoerd
156	Utopia Aalst (BE)	Dirk Verwoerd
158	Utopia Aalst (BE)	Rob Bruijnzeels
161	Utopia Aalst (BE)	Dirk Verwoerd
162-163	Utopia Aalst (BE)	Dirk Verwoerd
166	Michiel Riedijk	Renée Klein for Bibliotheekblad
168	Eemhuis Amersfoort (NL)	Daria Scagliola & Stijn Brakkee, Courtesy of Neutelings Riedijk
171	Eemhuis Amersfoort (NL)	Dirk Verwoerd
172-173	Eemhuis Amersfoort (NL)	Dirk Verwoerd
175	Rozet Arnhem (NL)	Courtesy of Neutelings Riedijk
177	Rozet Arnhem (NL)	Daria Scagliola & Stijn Brakkee, Courtesy of Neutelings Riedijk
178-179	Rozet Arnhem (NL)	Daria Scagliola en Stijn Brakkee, Courtesy of Neutelings Riedijk
180	Rozet Arnhem (NL)	Daria Scagliola en Stijn Brakkee, Courtesy of Neutelings Riedijk

Credits

Texts: Joyce Sternheim, Rob Bruijnzeels
Copy editing: Leo Reijnen
Translation: Jane Tee
Photo editing: Joyce Sternheim, Rob Bruijnzeels
Design: WOAU! Léon Kranenburg / Luigi Dorigoni
Printing and lithography: die Keure
Publisher: Marcel Witvoet, nai010 publishers

This publication was made possible with financial support from Creative Industries Fund NL and ekz benelux, ekz-Gruppe

© 2021 authors, nai010 publishers, Rotterdam.
All rights reserved. No part of this publication may be reproduced, stored in a retrieval system, or transmitted in any form or by any means, electronic, mechanical, photocopying, recording or otherwise, without the prior written permission of the publisher.

For works of visual artists affiliated with a CISAC-organization the copyrights have been settled with Pictoright in Amsterdam.
© 2021, c/o Pictoright Amsterdam

Although every effort was made to find the copyright holders for the illustrations used, it has not been possible to trace them all. Interested parties are requested to contact nai010 publishers, Korte Hoogstraat 31, 3011 GK Rotterdam, the Netherlands.

nai010 publishers is an internationally orientated publisher specialized in developing, producing and distributing books in the fields of architecture, urbanism, art and design.
www.nai010.com

nai010 books are available internationally at selected bookstores and from the following distribution partners:

North, Central and South America - Artbook | D.A.P., New York, USA, dap@dapinc.com

Rest of the world - Idea Books, Amsterdam, the Netherlands, idea@ideabooks.nl

For general questions, please contact nai010 publishers directly at sales@nai010.com or visit our website www.nai010.com for further information.

Printed and bound in Belgium

ISBN 978-94-6208-662-3
NUR 648
BISAC ARC011000, ARC000000

Imagination and Participation. Next Steps in Public Library Architecture
also available as e-book (pdf):
ISBN 978-94-6208-688-3 (e-book)